S0-AXZ-860

THE ART OF JEWELRY MAKING

CLASSIC & ORIGINAL DESIGNS

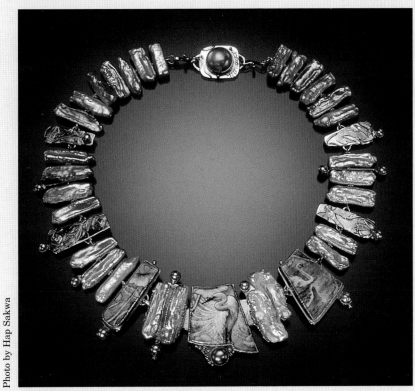

Photo by Hap Sakwa

HUNTER

ALAN REVERE

Sterling Publishing Co., Inc. New York
A Sterling/Chapelle Book

CHAPELLE LTD.

Owner
Jo Packham

Design/Layout Editor
Karmen Quinney

Staff
Marie Barber, Ann Bear,
Areta Bingham, Kass Burchett,
Rebecca Christensen, Brenda Doncouse,
Dana Durney, Marilyn Goff, Holly
Hollingsworth, Shawn Hsu,
Susan Jorgensen, Barbara Milburn,
Linda Orton, Leslie Ridenour,
Cindy Stoeckl, Gina Swapp

Photography
Barry Blau

Illustrations
George McLean

Technical Editor
Tim McCreight

Photo by Ralph Gabriner

CLARKSON

As you look through the images and read the words in this book, feel free to make the jewelry as presented and to experiment on your own. However, please understand that all items shown are protected by copyright. The makers have generously agreed to let you follow their steps so that you can replicate these items for your own use. However, the commercial reproduction and sale of items in this book are strictly forbidden.

Library of Congress Cataloging-in-Publication Data

10 9 8 7 6 5 4 3

First paperback edition published in 2001 by
Sterling Publishing Company, Inc.,
387 Park Avenue South, New York, NY 10016
© 1999 by Chapelle Limited
Distributed in Canada by Sterling Publishing
% Canadian Manda Group, One Atlantic Avenue, Suite 105
Toronto, Ontario, Canada M6K 3E7
Distributed in Great Britain by Chrysalis Books
64 Brewery Road, London N7 9NT, England
Distributed in Australia by Capricorn Link (Australia) Pty Ltd.
P.O. Box 704, Windsor, NSW 2756, Australia
Printed in China
All Rights Reserved

Sterling ISBN 0-8069-2070-X Trade
           0-8069-4767-5 Paper

If you have any questions or comments, please contact: Chapelle Ltd., Inc., P.O. Box 9252 Ogden, UT 84409 (801) 621-2777 • FAX (801) 621-2788 • E-mail Chapelle1@ aol.com

The written instructions, photographs, designs, patterns, and projects in this volume are intended for the personal use of the reader and may be reproduced for that purpose only. Any other use, especially commercial use, is forbidden under law without the written permission of the copyright holder. Every effort has been made to ensure that all of the information in this book is accurate.

Due to differing conditions, tools, and individual skills, the publisher cannot be responsible for any injuries, losses, and/or other damages which may result from the use of the information in this book.

Warning: Some of the procedures described in this book can be harmful if not executed properly. Neither the author nor the publisher assumes any liability for personal injury resulting from information that follows, whether accurate or not. Learn about the hazards of all techniques and materials before using them. Always wear protective goggles and use proper safety measures. Your safety is your responsibility. When in doubt, consult an expert first.

CONTENTS

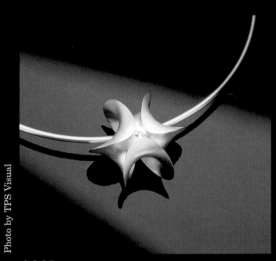

Photo by TPS Visual

GOOD

ALAN REVERE

Alan Revere holds a unique position within the jewelry community. With one foot firmly planted as an innovative designer and the other as one of the country's most prominent jewelry educators, Alan has built a national reputation as a leader in the jewelry industry.

Alan grew up in a family of visual artists. Although both grandfathers as well as his mother created art as a hobby for most of their lives, his family pushed him into academics and in 1969 he received a B. A. in psychology from the University of Virginia.

Opting to continue his education at Woodstock rather than law school, Alan pointed his Volkswagen bus south toward what he hoped would be artistic freedom in Mexico. He landed in the art colony of San Miguel de Allende, where for two years he studied drawing, sculpture, and crafts at the Instituto Allende. It was here that he was introduced to jewelry. "The first time I worked in silver, I knew I had found my medium," he recalls. "I had always been drawn to metal objects; coins, bottle caps, machine parts, etc. Jewelry offered an ideal outlet for my talents and interests. Working in precious metals and gems threw open a wide door of possibilities from the start." At about the same time, Alan fell in love and married a weaving student, Jean Mann.

Dedicated to the point that time became irrelevant, Alan frequently worked through the night at his bench, producing jewelry which sold as fast as he could make it. At that point, he realized that he needed the best possible training. With a Master of Fine Arts degree and a thousand dollars in hand, Revere, his wife, and their dog, moved to Pforzheim, Germany. For two more years he attended the Fachhochschule für Gestaltung, a hundred-year-old school with a worldwide reputation for turning out top notch jewelry designers.

Returning to the U.S., Alan opened his studio and established a school in San Francisco's historic jewelry building, where he works today. In addition to directing and teaching at the Revere Academy of Jewelry Arts, Alan has received a number of international awards for his jewelry designs. Alan is the author of articles, books, and video tapes on jewelry making, including *Professional Goldsmithing*, a book which many consider to be a modern classic on the traditional art of making jewelry.

Alan and Jean Revere live in Marin County with their daughter Alexis and three dogs. Their son, Dustin, is an artist/glass blower now exploring his own creativity and driving a Volkswagen bus.

Wheeeeel

INTRODUCTION

Jewelry making is a lot of things to a lot of people. For one, it is a very old art, especially if you include Adam's leaf as personal adornment. And if you are not willing to go that far, certainly a short time later Adam most likely twisted some grass around his finger and gave it to Eve, (or vice versa).

MESSINA

Jewelry fulfills many basic human needs—social, spiritual, economic, aesthetic, tactile, symbolic—and the list goes on. There is something very old, primordial, and mystical about jewelry and its creation. Neal Pollack expresses the feelings of many when he states, "After all these years, I still feel the same magic every time I sit down at the bench."

Jewelry making can be exhilarating, as Marianne Hunter discovered. "It offered me a euphoric sense of limitlessness."

Jewelry is a refined art form. "Every piece of my jewelry is an attempt to bring visual poetry into the world," says Michael Sugarman.

Jewelry is a complex craft. "I was fascinated by the paraphernalia, the minutia, the potential. I wanted to know what every tool did," recalls Jaclyn Davidson when she stepped into a jewelry workshop for the first time.

Jewelry making is a satisfying experience. "After 30 years at this craft, I still wake up eager to go to work in the morning," says David Clarkson.

Jewelry making offers a way for creative people to survive on their work. "I finally found something that I enjoyed doing, not just something that I had to do so that I could enjoy something else," says Ross Coppelman.

Jewelry making offers endless challenges. For Charles Lewton-Brain, "The best part about being a goldsmith is that every time I walk into the workshop there is something new to see or discover."

Jewelry impacts the way a maker views the world. "Jewelry became a vehicle for my investigation of technical and philosophical concepts with a far deeper meaning than mere personal adornment," says Michael Good.

Jewelry making offers the pleasures of discovery and creation with a never ending reservoir of rewards. "I am forever drawn in by the medium," Robert Pfuelb says. "Working with tools, metals, and gems pulls me back to my bench day after day after day, without ever being bored."

COPPELMAN

Jewelry represents love on several levels. The giving and wearing of jewelry conveys the message of love. Voicing the feelings of many, Patrick Murphy says simply, "I love what I do." Sam Brown says it in a different way, "I love each and every piece I make."

Come along as we survey 25 contemporary jewelry makers, and explore their relationships to jewelry. Each brings an individual outlook, artistry, and passion to their work. Each of these artists puts heart and soul into every piece. For those who endeavor to create in precious metals, including those whose work appears in the following pages, jewelry can be the ultimate blend of vocation and avocation. As Ross Coppelman observes, "Within jewelry, work and play became indistinguishable."

TOOLS

Tools are essential to most crafts, and they are especially important for making fine jewelry. No other craft requires as many individual tools as jewelry work. The old saying, "The right tool is half the job," is a jewelry truism. While it is possible to get started with just a few pieces of equipment and hand tools, you will find that as your skills and projects evolve, you will need more, and more tools.

There is a natural division between hand tools found at the bench, and the larger pieces of equipment found in a jewelry workshop. Here is a description of the most important hand tools, grouped loosely by function, found in a jewelry workshop:

Photo by Hap Sakwa

BROWN

Photo by Ralph Gabriner

DEAN

Safety — Research all materials and procedures. If you have any doubt about the safety of a procedure, do not do it. Learn to use tools before trying them. Remember that your safety is your responsibility.

Optivisors and loupes — These magnification tools come in different types.

Goggles and face shield — Wear the correct device to protect your eyes and face from flying particles, dust, sparks, and hazardous chemicals when working in any kind of shop.

Platinum goggles — These are required and specially rated for working with platinum.

Dust masks and respirators — These devices protect the wearer from hazard during operations that produce dust or fumes.

HOLDING TOOLS

Jewelry is composed of small, odd-sized components that must be held securely and safely for filing, sawing, drilling, setting, bending, etc.

Pin vises (A) — hold wire during filing, drill bits during sharpening, and tubing during setting.

Ring clamp (B) — holds rings and other small, noncrushable items firmly.

Inside/outside ring clamp (C) — exposes the entire outer surface for operations like setting, filing, and engraving.

Tweezers (D) — pick up and hold all kinds of small objects, sometimes during soldering.

Tube holder (E) — accepts rods and tubes for setting, filing, sawing, etc.

Large hand vise (F) — holds larger and less delicate items for filing, bending, sanding, sawing, etc.

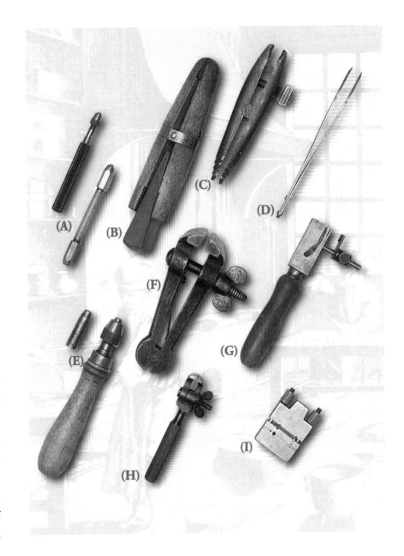

Tube cutting jig (G) — holds a piece of tubing, wire, or rod at a fixed length during sawing or filing. A clamp secures the piece as the saw blade slips through a guide to cut flat and straight.

Small hand vise (H) — holds smaller items securely for many operations.

Precision filing block (I) — holds small pieces of sheet, wire, or tubing for precision sawing, filing, and bending at 45° and 90°.

PLIERS

There is a nearly endless array of pliers for holding every conceivable shape of object.

Metal snips (A) — cut thin sheet metal and solder. Heavier-duty models are also available.

Ring holding pliers (B) — hold a ring securely when filing, sanding, burring, or polishing the inside.

Parallel pliers (C) — help hold larger and thicker material without marring the surface.

End cutting nippers (D) — cut small pieces of wire.

Round-nose pliers (E) — have two long conical jaws, enabling one to bend tight curves in wire and sheet.

Half-round pliers (F) — bend sheet or wire into smooth curves when making ring shanks, bezels, etc.

Chain-nose pliers (G) — hold smaller objects, such as jump rings. They are like flat pliers, but with jaws that taper toward the tip.

Flat pliers (H) — used to hold sheet and wire. These are probably the most important pliers.

Small flat pliers (I) — handy for smaller pieces of material.

Slide-locking pliers (J) — grip like a small hand vise or heavy-duty pliers. These are sturdy flat pliers with teeth and a metal slide to lock the jaws.

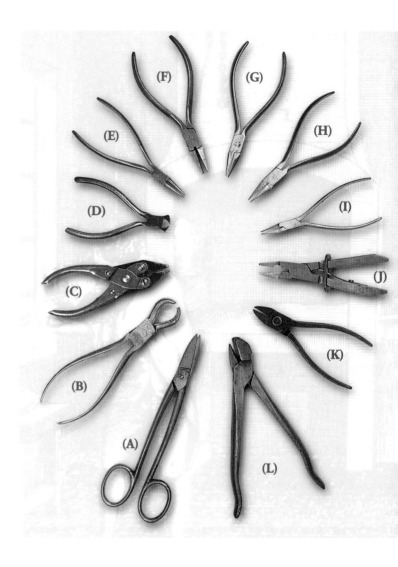

Side cutting nippers (K) — similar to the end cutters. This is a heavier-duty pair of cutters.

Ring bending (bow closing) pliers (L) — offer high leverage for difficult bending. Make a thin copper hood for the two-pronged jaw to protect the work against marring.

MEASURING AND LAYOUT TOOLS

The most critical step in building anything, (whether it is a ring or a skyscraper) is the first step —layout. Everything that follows depends on the accuracy of measuring and layout that occurs before the first operation is even begun.

Ring sizers (A) — measure fingers in half-size increments.

Small machinist's square (B) — provides a guide for scribing lines on metal as well as for checking the flatness of surfaces, and accuracy of right angles.

Digital caliper (C) — measures thickness, inside distance, and depth. This model displays measurements in hundredths of a millimeter or thousandths of an inch.

Metric ruler (D) — used for measuring and layout.

Dividers (E) — used to lay out straight lines and circles and transfer measurements.

Machinist's protractor (F) — measures angles and provides a straight edge for layout.

Center punch (G) — struck by a hammer to make an indentation as a guide for drilling.

Scribe (H) — scratches layout lines onto metal.

Brass slide caliper (I) — useful caliper alternative. This model fits in your pocket. Be certain it has a vernier scale so that you can read tenths of a millimeter or sixteenths of an inch.

Dial caliper (J) — easy to read. This plastic model is highly functional.

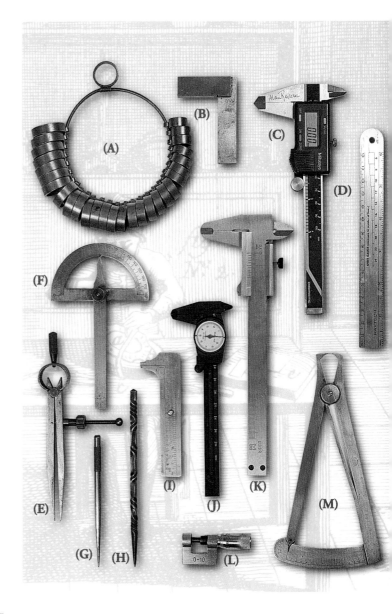

Vernier caliper (K) — durable and accurate standard steel model.

Micrometer (L) — determines the thickness of wire and sheet.

Spring gauge (M) — measures the thickness of metal. It is especially useful where there is limited access.

CUTTING TOOLS

Metal can be cut and carved by sanding, sawing, filing, and engraving.

Sanding stick (A) — made by wrapping abrasive paper around a wooden paint stick.

Jeweler's saw frame (B) — (See Sawing on page 16.) used for sawing, piercing, precision filing, and even limited engraving.

Saw blades (C) — available in a variety of sizes.

Needle files (D) — available in a multitude of shapes and sizes.

Gravers (E) — (See Engraving on page 16.) carve metal, set stones, and apply surface ornamentation. These are traditional push chisels.

Triangle scraper (F) — removes burs.

Small barrette file (G) — excellent for smaller jobs. The bottom of the file has a flat cutting surface.

Crossing file (H) — has two different curved cutting surfaces.

Inside ring file (I) — fits inside all but the smallest rings.

Barrette file (J) — here is the full-size version.

Flat file (K) — has a rectangular cross section with cutting surfaces on three or four sides

Square file (L) — creases metal so that it can be folded to a 90° angle.

Round file (M) — used on the inside of tight curves.

Half-round file (N) — offers both flat and curved cutting surfaces.

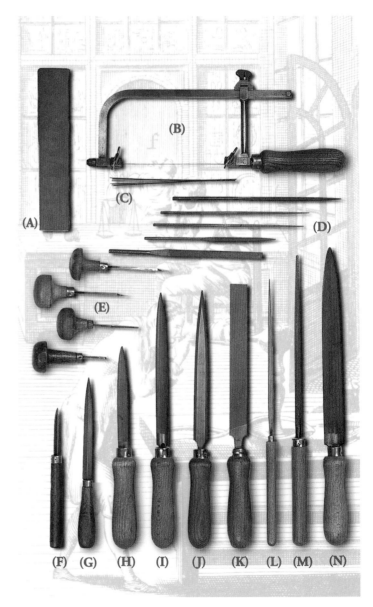

HAMMERS

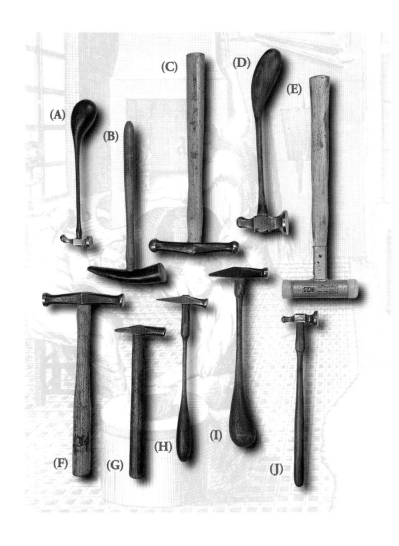

Hammering is one of the most ancient ways to form metal. Here are a few basic hammers, each of which comes in a range of sizes and variations.

Chasing hammer (A) — strikes punches and other steel tools. The ball end can be used for embossing. This mini version was made by Abrasha. (See Abrasha on page 21.) It is ideal for delicate work like stone setting and chasing.

Horn mallet (B) — forms metal without marring the surface.

Forming hammer (C) — shapes metal with spherical ends in two sizes. Use it for forming, embossing, or forging metal.

Chasing hammer (D) — strikes center punches, dapping punches, bezel punches, repoussé punches, and other large steel tools.

Dead-blow mallet (E) — made with two hard, plastic heads and filled with steel shot to eliminate the recoil.

Planishing hammer (F) — used for forming, forging, flattening, and texturing.

Goldsmithing hammer (G) — strikes jewelry metals. It has a slightly domed face on one side and a cross peen on the other. This small yet hefty model has a cross peen and a higher-than-average dome.

Goldsmithing hammer (H) — used for fine work, with a narrow cross peen for riveting, and a lower dome.

Goldsmithing hammer (I) — (See Forging on page 19.) used for general work, with a medium cross peen and low dome for forging, flattening, shaping, riveting, etc.

Chasing hammer (J) — a midsize version, excellent for stone setting, chasing.

FORMING TOOLS

Most of these provide the form against which metal is shaped.

Agate burnisher (A) — hand-polishes metal components.

Pusher for setting (B) — pushes prongs and bezels over stones.

Burnisher (C) — helpful for setting bezels and polishing metal.

Bezel roller (D) — offers leverage to close a bezel over a stone.

Setting punch (E) — held in one hand while struck by a hammer held in the other.

Bezel block and punch (F) — are available in many shapes. These are used to form bezels.

Swage block (design block) (G) — forms metal, as in furrowing a tube blank.

Dapping block (H) — used with a set of complementary punches to form domes, hemispheres, and other similar shapes in metal. The shafts are used to form metal into cylindrical forms.

Bracelet mandrel (I) — used to form a bracelet. There are two basic styles, round and oval.

Ring mandrel (J) — used for forming rings and other curved shapes.

Oval bezel mandrel (K) — available in many shapes.

Round bezel mandrel (L) — used for forming bezels and cylinders.

Bench knife (M) — serves as a utility tool for prying, scraping, cutting, etc.

Anvil (N) — (See Forging on page 19.) flattens, forms, and forges small pieces of metal. One horn is conical and the other is pyramidal.

Bench brush (O) — cleans gold and silver dust off hands, work, and bench pin.

HEATING TOOLS

Heat is an essential part of jewelry making. It is used to alloy, cast, recycle, texture, solder, and join metals.

Copper tongs (A) — used in the pickle bath after soldering.

Open ingot mold (B) — used as a form for molten metal. Metal is heated to a liquid, then poured into this steel mold.

Crucible (C) — used for melting metal.

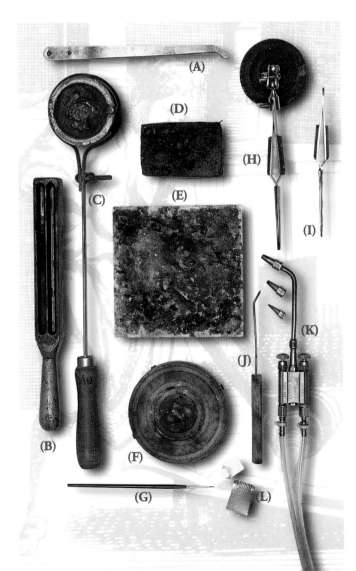

Charcoal block (D) — (See Soldering on page 17.) provides a soldering surface with a reducing atmosphere that absorbs oxygen during heating. It holds heat well for overall warming.

Refractory pad (E) — (See Soldering on page 17.) withstands and reflects the heat of soldering and heating. Both this and the charcoal block can be shaped and used to accept sharp pins for stabilizing the work.

Refractory turntable (F) — used for viewing and heating all around an object during soldering.

Flux brush (G) — applies flux and transports solder snippets.

Third hand (H) — holds metal in place during soldering.

Soldering tweezers (I) — place or hand-hold an item in position while soldering.

Solder pick (J) — made from a piece of steel, welding rod, titanium, etc., often mounted on a wooden handle. This tool is used to move solder into place, nudge metal into position, scrape oxides from seams, spread molten solder, pick-up, and place solder, etc.

Torch (K) — (See Soldering on page 17.) comes in different types. Selection of torches, tips, and fuel depends upon the work you are doing, the accessibility of fuel sources, and budget.

Solder (L) — flows before the metal components to join them together. It is an alloy of similar content to the metal being used for fabrication, but with a lower melting temperature.

DRAWING TOOLS

Wire, tubing, and some chains can be reduced in size and transformed into nearly any shape with draw plates. These hardened steel plates contain precision, graduated-tapered holes. Draw plates are mounted in a bench vise or draw bench to secure them while drawing materials through them.

Square draw plate (A) — used for creating or reducing the size of square wire.

Round draw plate (B) — (See Drawing on page 18.) used for creating or reducing the size of round wire.

Small round draw plate (C) — used for creating or reducing the size of small round wire.

Wooden draw plate (D) — used for drawing chain when you do not want the edges of the links to be flattened.

Rectangular draw plate (E) — used for creating or reducing the size of rectangular wire.

Draw tongs (F) — (See Drawing on page 18.) securely grips wire, tubing, and chains when pulling them through draw plates.

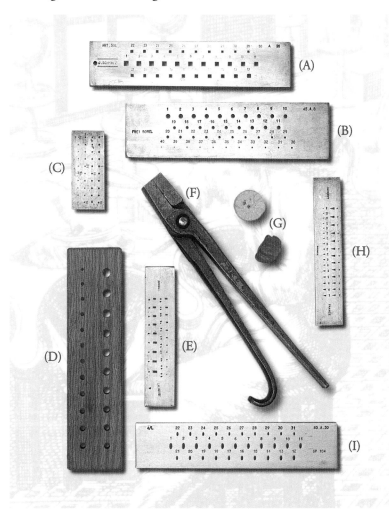

Lubricating waxes (G) — used to reduce friction when drawing.

Knife wire draw plate (H) — used for creating or reducing the size of knife wire (wire with a tall isosceles triangle cross section.)

Oval draw plate (I) — used for creating or reducing the size of oval wire.

FLEX-SHAFT AND FINISHING TOOLS

The appearance of a piece of jewelry is dependent largely on its finish. While a number of textures can be applied to metal, traditionally most surfaces are brought to a high polish.

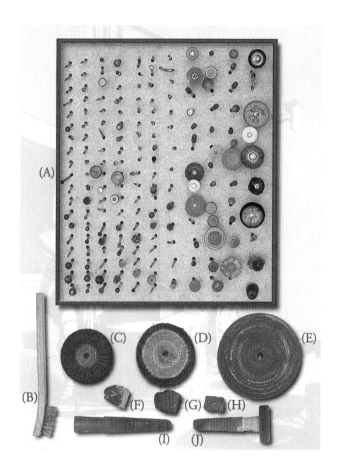

Flex-shaft tools (A) — come in a wide selection of small burs, buffs, wheels, cutters, drills, cutting discs, etc., and are used in the flexible-shaft machine. These come in a limitless variety of shapes, patterns, grits, sizes, and qualities, depending on the requirements for specific applications. Avoid overheating steel burs by lubricating with wax, oil, or soap. ALWAYS WEAR PROTECTIVE GOGGLES and dust masks when working with spinning tools that emit small particles.

Brass brush (B) — used with soapy water to apply a bright satin finish to metal.

Bristle brush (C) — available in a range of stiffness and sizes. These wheels are charged with compounds and used to reach into finely detailed areas.

Stitched muslin buff (D) — used for buffing and polishing jewelry with all compounds.

Hard felt wheel (E) — unlike the other wheels, these are often charged with compound on the sides, for buffing and polishing flat surfaces.

Bobbing compound (F) — used as a prepolishing (buffing) medium, this compound is coarse and abrasive.

Red rouge (G) — used to achieve a high luster on gold, silver, brass, and copper.

Green rouge (H) — used to apply a high shine to white metals — white gold, nickel, and platinum.

Inside ring buff (I) — used inside rings. These hard tapered buffs are charged with compounds since ordinary wheels cannot reach the interior of rings.

Combination felt buff (J) — consists of a small wheel and an inside ring buff combined into one for convenience.

PROCEDURES

In addition to utilizing a great variety of tools, jewelry making employs an immense diversity of techniques.

Filing — The bench pin is used as a support. Keep your arm and hand straight and in line with the file. Sanding with abrasive sticks is done the same way.

Bending — Pliers are generally used to bend wire and small pieces of sheet. Larger pieces of metal can be bent by pushing them into or around other forms: into a design block, around a vise jaw, around a mandrel, etc.

Shearing — Steel snips or shears are used to cut sheet and wire, much like scissors are used to cut paper. If the metal is too thick, it can be cut with a bench shear.

Annealing — Jewelry metals become harder when hammered, rolled, drawn, bent, etc. If worked too far, cracking will occur. Gold and silver can be rendered more workable by annealing, heating, then quenching in water.

Filing

Sawing

Sawing — This is one of the most basic operations. Most often the work is supported on the bench pin, as a saw with a very small blade is guided through the metal.

Engraving — Another very old technique of surface embellishment is engraving. This is the incising of lines and patterns into metal with gravers. The work is held securely in an engraving block or on a stick held up to the bench pin. Gravers are then used to carve or inscribe lines and patterns. Gravers are also used in stone setting techniques, like pavé and channel setting.

Engraving

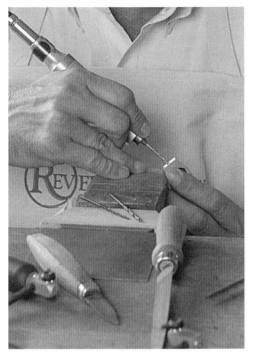
Drilling

Drilling, burring, grinding, etc. — All of these take place primarily with the work supported on the bench pin. A flexible-shaft machine provides the rotary action. The hand piece accepts a variety of little rotating cutters, drills, abrasives, etc. ALWAYS WEAR GOGGLES when using rotary tools. Stabilize the work on the bench pin with one hand. The other holds the hand piece and guides the tool as a foot pedal is used to control the speed.

Soldering — A torch provides the heat by sustaining the combustion of a fuel, such as propane or natural gas, mixed with air or oxygen. Separate valves enable one to produce a very controlled flame. More fuel results in a softer, cooler reducing flame, ideal for annealing and heating larger objects. Adding air or oxygen results in a smaller and hotter oxidizing flame, useful for small operations, such as soldering a chain and assembling small parts.

Soldering theory — Two pieces of metal can be joined by flowing a small amount of a lower melting temperature metal between them. Prior to soldering, the metals must be clean, fitted well together, and fluxed. Flux is a chemical that acts like glass in that it flows over the surface and seals it from the atmosphere, providing a coating under which the solder can flow without oxidation. Here are a few basic rules about soldering:
• Solder flows only on clean and fluxed metal.
• Solder flows toward the heat.
• Solder flows with gravity.
• Solder that is heated too high or too long absorbs gases and becomes pitted.

Soldering

Using solder — Solders come in a range of grades (melting temperatures) for all alloys: 14k yellow gold hard, medium, easy, etc. In complex assemblies, begin with hard solder, which has the highest temperature, and then subsequently use medium solder. If more work needs to be done nearby, use easy solder. Solder can be applied as snippets, prior to heating. It can be fed as wire into a hot seam. Solder snippets also can be fluxed and then fused on a charcoal block. When the metal balls up, a solder pick can be used to transport and place it onto a cold seam or feed it directly into a hot seam. The technique where one surface is coated with solder before it is brought in contact with another is called sweat soldering. When the two are heated together, the solder melts and joins them. *Note: In preparation for soldering, the components can be held in place by a number of ways. They can be tied together with binding wire, held in place with a third hand, or clipped together with U-shaped pieces of steel, like paper clips.*

Drawing — The diameter of wire is reduced by drawing it through graduated holes in a draw plate. Tubing can be made or reduced by using draw plates. The end of the material is tapered in preparation for drawing, and then it is fed through a hole in the draw plate. Draw tongs are used to pull as it is compressed and lengthened. Nearly any shape of wire can be created with the appropriate draw plate.

Drawing

Fusing — In lieu of soldering, metal components can be fused together by controlled melting at their contact points. (The temperature is above soldering range.) Flux is used to protect the surfaces and promote the process. Fusing results in a uniform piece of metal, without visible seams. Fused work usually has a natural and organic look. You can solder after fusing, but not vice versa.

Reticulation — It is possible with torch control, to actually melt the interior of a piece of metal sheet, without disturbing the outer surface. When this occurs the interior pulls and flows so that the skin changes texture and shape.

Fire coating — Sometimes, if left unprotected, the surface of heated metal oxidizes and becomes stained. This can be prevented by coating the piece or assembly in a solution of boric acid powder and alcohol. The alcohol carries the boric acid. It is then ignited, leaving a powdered coating on the surface. When heated, this boric acid powder works like flux to seal the surface and protect it. It also protects polished surfaces during soldering.

Casting — Perhaps the most basic way of working with metal is to heat it until it is a liquid, then pour it into a container that can endure the heat. When the metal freezes, it takes on the shape of the container. This is casting, an ancient technique that is still the basis for much jewelry work around the world, from one-of-a-kind studio work to mass production. There are several types of casting, but the most popular in jewelry is lost-wax casting. Here are the basic steps:

- Create a wax model by carving, building up, or injecting wax into a mold.
- Sprue the model onto a wax "tree" that will provide a channel for the molten metal.
- Mount the tree onto a sprue base.
- Invest the sprued model. The item is put into a flask and covered completely with investment, a type of plaster that can withstand lots of heat.
- Cure the investment by allowing it to fully harden.
- Burn out the flask. Heat it to melt out the wax model, leaving an empty chamber duplicating the shape of the object, then raise the temperature close to that of the molten metal.
- Melt the metal in a crucible.
- Pour molten metal into the cavity.
- Quench the flask in water.
- Remove the metal model as the investment breaks apart.

The most popular casting machines are centrifuges. A centrifugal casting machine spins fast so that the molten metal is pushed into all details in the cavity. Another popular method is vacuum casting. In this system the metal is "sucked" into the chamber by a vacuum that pulls through the porous investment so that the liquid metal fills the cavity quickly. Other methods of casting include ingot casting, sand casting, charcoal casting, cuttlefish casting, stone casting, and pouring molten metal onto water, ice, straw, brick, etc. An advantage of casting is that nearly any shape can be carved in wax and then cast. Casting is economical for producing multiples.

Fabrication — This is the method of constructing items directly in sheet and wire.

Forming — when metal is shaped without significantly disturbing the thickness, it is called forming. Examples include dapping, bending, folding, embossing, hydraulic die forming, anticlastic raising, etc.

Forging — when the cross section or thickness of metal is altered by striking with hammers.

Forging

Riveting — Sometimes metal parts are "cold joined" by pinning them together rather than by soldering.

Rolling — This procedure reduces the thickness of sheet and wire. A rolling mill has two hardened steel cylinders that squeeze a piece of metal to make it thinner. The rolls are brought closer together and it is rolled again to reduce it further. Flat rollers are for sheet. Grooved rollers are for wire.

Roll printing — A piece of metal sheet can be pressed into a textured surface, using a rolling mill. Make a sandwich of brass sheet, texture, annealed metal, and more brass. Adjust the pressure and roll it through so that the texture transfers. Nearly any texture can be used—cloth, leaves, metal screen, etched metal, etc.

Pickling — After soldering, fusing, or annealing, the work is immersed in a warm, weak acid bath called a pickle that removes the flux, oxides, and tarnish.

Fold-forming — (See Charles Lewton-Brain on page 96.)

Hydraulic pressing — (See Robert Grey Kaylor on page 25.)

Enameling — An ancient technique whereby powdered glass or pieces of colored glass are applied to a metal surface, which is then heated. When the enamel melts, it flows over the surface. Enamels come in many colors. Some are opaque, some are transparent, and some are translucent. All enamels are fragile. Lead-free enamels are replacing traditional lead-bearing enamels for health reasons. Enameling requires careful planning and extreme cleanliness.

Rolling

Buffing and polishing — A high luster can be applied to most metals by buffing, prepolishing, and polishing. Buffing is the first stage in which fine sanding lines or other surface unevenness are abraded by cutting compounds charged onto cloth wheels mounted on the spindles of a polishing lathe. After buffing, the work is cleaned in an ultrasonic bath and steamed to remove all dirt and compound residue. Then the surface can be brought to a higher luster, using a polishing compound on a separate wheel. Great care must be taken to protect eyes and mouth. Tie back loose clothing and long hair for safety.

ABRASHA

Born in Holland to Polish parents and trained in Germany, Abrasha moved to the United States where he met and married an Italian woman. International in outlook and in style, Abrasha (who dropped his last name long ago) has established himself as an avant-garde designer among collectors and as a master technician among his peers.

Photo by Nici Groth

"I am strongly influenced by the Bauhaus movement and Japanese design, both of which share a strong sense of simplicity," Abrasha states. "At school and work in Germany, I learned a very high level of precision which has always been the cornerstone of my jewelry. But precision is only the vehicle for the ideas I see in my mind."

Abrasha's work is contemporary, geometric, and simple in style. He is a purist

who uses high karat gold alloys, which he prepares himself along with stainless steel, platinum, silver, and fine gems. He often combines these with unconventional materials and found objects, such as discarded CO_2 cartridges, pachinko balls, stainless or rusted steel, and plywood. All of his work is painstakingly hand-fabricated. "I usually combine two or three different materials to create tension between their texture, value, and colors in my designs," says the artist.

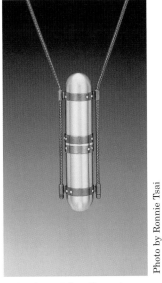

Photo by Ronnie Tsai

CO2 Cartridge Container

A signature feature of Abrasha's work is the use of small rivets to hold pieces together. In addition to their function, these precious little fasteners are an important visual design element. Often slightly irregular in shape and placement, they offer a humanistic counter-point to the machinesque geometry, which is the basis of his work. In addition to its wearability and visual appeal, Abrasha's work is highly collectable. He has taken part in dozens of international competitions and exhibitions. His jewelry is included in the permanent collection of the Smithsonian Museum's Renwick Gallery as well as the California Crafts Collection at the Oakland Museum.

Always on the forefront of design and technology, Abrasha has most recently incorporated a computer to design and a lathe to create his jewelry and ornamental objects. Looking forward, Abrasha reflects, "The future is not ours to see until it is past. Much of my work captures contemporary materials in precious metal settings in a manner that will insure their visibility in the future."

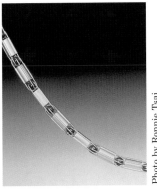

Photo by Ronnie Tsai

Rusty Ball Necklace

WASHER RING

Photo by Ronnie Tsai

Although the finest jewelry is still made by hand, the line between hand and machine craftsmanship blurs as technologies advance. Abrasha's fascination with technology supports the machine-like qualities in his work. This unusual ring was conceived and created at confluence of hand and machine.

WASHER RING

Materials		Measurements
	Stainless steel rod in alloy #303	1¾" diameter
24k	Gold sheet	0.5 mm (24 gauge) x 8.2 mm
24k	Gold square wire	0.9 mm (19 gauge)
24k	Gold round wire	1 mm (18 gauge)
	Sterling silver sheet	0.6 mm (22 gauge)

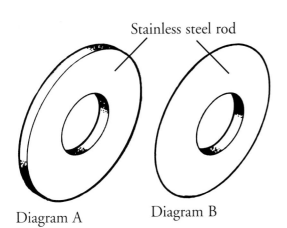

Stainless steel rod

Diagram A

Diagram B

24k gold sheet

Diagram C

Diagram D

Sterling silver

Diagram E

24k gold square wire

24k gold
square wire

Diagram F

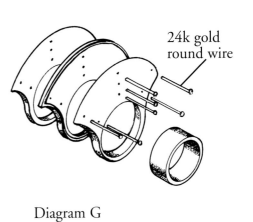

24k gold
round wire

Diagram G

WASHER RING

1 Using a lathe, machine two 3 mm thick washers from the stainless steel rod with an outside diameter of 44 mm and an inside diameter of 17.5 mm. (See Diagram A on page 23.)

2 Machine the washers so that they are convex on one side, by placing them in a specially made holding jig held in the lathe chuck. (See Diagram B on page 23.)

3 Make a sleeve from 24k gold sheet with a thickness of 0.5 mm, that has the desired ring size and is 8.2 mm tall. (See Diagram C on page 23.)

4 Bore out the inside holes of the washers to fit the gold sleeve. Chamfer (counter-sink) the holes on the convex side at 45°. Layout the ring's outline onto the two washers. Saw and file the outer shape making the two washers identical. (See Diagram D on page 23.)

5 Trace the outlines of the steel parts onto the sterling silver sheet and then trim the lines 0.3 mm in from the edges.

6 On the silver blank, locate, center punch, and drill holes for rivets with a 0.8 mm bit. (See Diagram E on page 23.)

7 Form the 24k gold square wire, 0.9 mm thick, around the silver blank. Solder with medium silver solder. Forge the gold rim to the same thickness as the silver. Sand flat. (See Diagram F on page 23.)

Necklace

Photo by Ronnie Tsai

8 Assemble the gold sleeve, the gold/silver blank, and one of the steel sides. Drill rivet holes into one steel side with the silver blank as a guide. Add the second steel side to the assembly. Drill the rivet holes into this part, using the already drilled holes in the first steel side and the silver blank as guides. Take the assembly apart.

9 Clean up and counter sink the rivet holes on the outside of the steel pieces. Assemble the parts. (See Diagram G on page 23.)

10 Hold the 1 mm gold round wire in tweezers and heat to fuse and "ball up" the end. Cut 10 mm long. Repeat this process until you have seven sphere-headed rivets. Insert the rivets. Use a cross peen to upset the plain ends, forcing them into the counter-sunk recesses in the steel.

11 Flare the ends of the 24k gold ring sleeve outward against the chamfers in the stainless steel side plates, pressing the gold against the 45° bevels made earlier. Hammer the 24k gold rim on the silver section over the steel side plates. File off excess. Sand and finish ring.

ROBERT GREY KAYLOR

Fold-formed Pendant

Photo by Ralph Gabriner

Being independent comes easy for Robert Grey Kaylor. He grew up in a small midwestern town and has been on his own since age sixteen. Unaware of the role art would play in his life, Robert lived in his first creation, an old Rambler station wagon with the Zig-Zag™ man painted on the doors. Before graduating from high school, Robert loaded his belongings into his car and headed west. He ended up in Flagstaff, Arizona, where he landed a job in a sawmill.

One Saturday afternoon at a market, Robert discovered a Navajo man selling silver and turquoise jewelry. He had never really thought much about jewelry, but watching the craftsman work struck a deep resonance within him. Within weeks Robert had assembled some tools and set up a very crude jewelry shop in his apartment. A few days later, he made his first ring and he wore it with pride. Returning to the market a month later, Robert asked the Navajo to show him how to make jewelry and to Robert's surprise the man offered to teach him in the evenings. Robert developed a small client base and started to take classes in jewelry at Northern Arizona University.

When the bottom fell out of the silver and turquoise market, Robert once again packed his belongings and hit the road—this time winding up in Boise, Idaho. He began as a goldsmith's apprentice, then graduated to doing repairs for local jewelry stores. He eventually opened his own small store, specializing in custom design. These days, Robert can be found in a large elegant jewelry gallery, which he runs with his wife Barbara. Although they also represent dozens of contemporary designers, Robert's work is the centerpiece of the establishment.

With as many twists and turns as his career has provided, one thing has become clear to Robert. "A long time ago, I realized that it was essential to stay open to change," he says. "Standing in one place for too long means stagnation." Ever the student of new ideas, Robert has taken advantage of the national jewelry workshop scene. In one workshop, Robert was introduced to the Bonny Doon hydraulic press. In another, he learned the in's and out's of fold forming. "I have integrated both of these techniques into my work, he says. "One is mechanical and the other is all hands on. Together, they have expanded the envelope of my work into directions I could have never imagined only a few years ago." As committed to fostering change in others as in himself, Robert says, "As an artist, I accept the responsibility for always bringing fresh ideas into the world."

Photo by Deborah Hardee

Photo by Robert Grey Kaylor

HYDRAULICALLY FORMED CUFF BRACELET

Although there is little new in the world of jewelry making, in recent years new technologies have been brought into the small jewelry workshop. Using a hydraulic press, opens new worlds for the studio jeweler. This elegant yet simple bracelet demonstrates one possibility of hydraulic forming in precious metals.

HYDRAULICALLY FORMED CUFF BRACELET

Materials	Measurements
Sterling silver sheet	1 mm (18 gauge)
Sterling silver half-round wire	3.3 mm (8 gauge)
Copper sheet	1.3 mm (16 gauge)

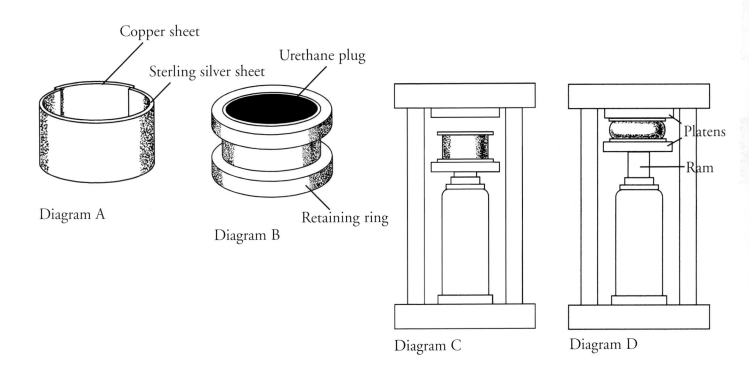

Copper sheet

Sterling silver sheet

Diagram A

Urethane plug

Retaining ring

Diagram B

Diagram C

Platens

Ram

Diagram D

Diagram E

Sterling silver
half-round wire

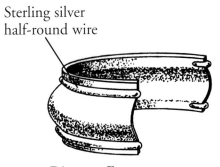

Diagram F

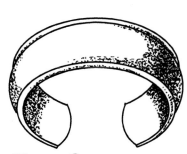

Diagram G

HYDRAULICALLY FORMED CUFF BRACELET

1 Begin with an annealed piece or 1 mm sterling silver sheet that is 15.2 cm long and 7.5 cm wide. Overlapping the edge of the sheet, solder on a piece of 1.3 mm copper sheet that is 8.4 cm long and 7.5 mm wide. The overlapping joints add strength to resist the tremendous force of hydraulic forming. Round the bracelet into a cylinder over a large mandrel. (See Diagram A on page 27.)

2 A urethane plug is required for forming the bracelet. It should fit snugly inside the cylinder. Add two retaining rings at the top and bottom, outside the cylinder. These can be made of heavy gauge square brass rod, approximately 4–6 mm per side, joined with overlapping seams or scarf joints. *Note: A scarf joint has two long diagonal faces which add strength to the bond. If needed, tape the parts in position on the outside.* (See Diagram B on page 27.)

3 Insert the assembly between the platens of a twenty-ton hydraulic press. Presses with an electric pump make light work of cranking the pressure up. (See Diagram C on page 27.)

4 Add hydraulic pressure, which raises the ram. This crushes the cylinder and forces the urethane outward in the middle of the cylinder while retaining rings hold the ends in place. As more pressure is applied, pay close attention to the seams. If one rips open, stop and repair it. Annealing may be needed to avoid ripping. Continue to form the metal until the desired bulge is achieved. (See Diagram D on page 27.)

5 Release the pressure, lower the ram and remove the assembly. The urethane should slide out with a little force. (See Diagram E on page 27.)

6 Cut the copper section of the bracelet in order to separate and remove the retaining rings. String a saw blade through the center of the cylinder and cut outwards until you break through the copper. Drill a hole and complete the cut by stringing the blade between rings.

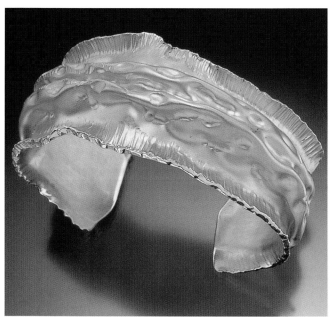

Hydraulically Raised Cuff Bracelet

Photo by Robert Grey Kaylor

7 Compress the bracelet and slide off the rings. Trim away the copper from the silver and correct for desired wrist size. Anneal the bracelet and spread the ends so that it has a slightly larger diameter. Prepare the edges for soldering.

8 Cut two pieces of half-round sterling silver wire, 3.3 mm diameter and 16.5 cm long. Anneal and form around a large mandrel to match the shape of the bracelet, where the retaining rings once were. Wrap the wires around the bracelet next to the bulge and pull them snug. Crimp the ends over the edges of the bracelet, locking the wires in place. Forcing the bracelet closed again tightens the fit of the half-round wire bands. (See Diagram F on page 27.)

9 Firecoat the entire piece in boric acid and alcohol to retard oxidation and the build-up of firescale during soldering. Flux the seams and place small snippets of solder all around the seam on the outside edge. Solder the two wire bands in place. Pickle and clean the metal.

10 Saw and file the sides of the bracelet, removing the metal beyond the half-round wire. Saw and file the ends of the bracelet as well, removing the crimped ends of the wire and making certain there are no sharp corners.

11 Use a bead blaster to add a soft texture all over, then polish the half-round edges for contrast. (See Diagram G on page 27.)

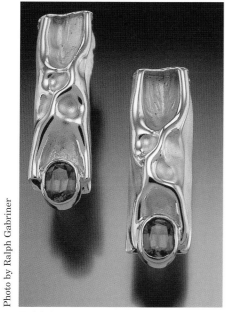

Photo by Ralph Gabriner

Fold-formed Earrings

Photo by Ralph Gabriner

Hydraulically Raised and Fold-formed Earrings

TAMI DEAN

Photo by Shannon Spence

Tami Dean has an innate need to keep her hands busy. So, when she was preparing to trek through Peru and Bolivia in the early 80's, she put a tiny embroidery hoop in her backpack. "It served as an anchor for my identity," she says. "During a journey of amazing adventures, whether on a steamy Amazonian boat ride or hiking on chilly oxygen-spare mountains, it was my embroidery that tied me to reality." Surprisingly, it was in this region of the world that Tami's fascination with metals was born. However, it was not jewelry that turned her head. Instead it was the unexpected stimulation she found in Latin American hardware; specifically the design and function of fasteners, locks, and hinges.

"When I returned, I was eager to learn to make hardware," the artist recalls. So, Tami enrolled in a metals program at the Oregon College of Arts and Crafts. "To my surprise, I became completely engrossed in jewelry and at the end of my first term the head of the Metals Department, Joe Apodaca, agreed to take me on as his apprentice." Tami spent the next two years working under this highly-skilled jewelry designer. It was just the impetus she needed to catapult her into a career of metal jewelry.

"I discovered that the scale of jewelry was close to that of the embroidery which I loved," Tami says of her early experiences in jewelry. "I was challenged by the added parameters of wearability and I became fascinated by the magic of well-finished minutia." It is this attention to design detail at several levels that marks the work of Tami Dean. Tami has developed a vocabulary of her own, composed of triangles, dots, and swirls used as accents to balance the overall grace in her work.

Aphrodite Necklace   Photo by Hap Sakwa

Tami has recently expanded into a totally unexpected niche embellishing the trumpets of such world-class musicians as Wynton Marsalis, Art Farmer, and Ron Miles. Stepping back, Tami admits, "I accept the responsibility to make "good work" worthy of the venerable materials from which I am privileged to create." Although well aware of the intrinsic value of her materials, Tami strives to achieve a greater import based on the marks left by the hands of the artist.

Here are three similar rings, which can be used as wedding bands. Each is encircled by a continuous pierced and appliquéd design. The spontaneity of the piercing balances the weight of the appliqué elements.

Photo by Ralph Gabriner

WHITE AND YELLOW GOLD WEDDING BANDS

Materials		*Measurements*
14k	Yellow gold sheet	1.2 mm (17 gauge), 6.5 mm wide
14k	Palladium white gold sheet	0.6 mm (22 gauge)

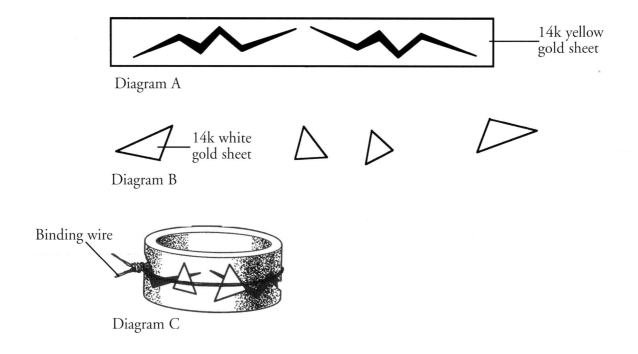

Diagram A — 14k yellow gold sheet

Diagram B — 14k white gold sheet

Diagram C — Binding wire

WHITE AND YELLOW GOLD WEDDING BANDS

1 Begin with the yellow gold sheet, and cut it to 57.8 mm for a size 7 ring.

2 Rough up the surface with an abrasive pad, raising a "tooth" to hold penciled designs. Use a sharp mechanical pencil to freehand the design on the ring blank. Incorporate one overlay element that will cover the solder seam.

3 Drill a small starter hole and pierce the design, using 6/0 and 4/0 saw blades. (See Diagram A on page 32.) Clean up the cut-outs, using needle files.

4 Stamp the blank with a maker's mark and 14k yellow gold.

5 Bend the ring into a rough circle, using ring bending pliers. Although the shape is unimportant at this point, the ends must meet evenly and squarely with tension.

6 Solder with yellow gold hard solder and pickle; rinse and dry.

7 Round the band with a mallet over a ring mandrel. File and sand to smooth the surfaces.

8 Flow yellow gold easy solder onto the back of the white gold sheet. The solder is melted onto the surface and spread while hot, using a solder pick, until an even layer covers the metal.

9 Cut out the desired white gold shapes, using shears or a jeweler's saw. (See Diagram B on page 32.) Form the pieces to match the contour of the band by placing them into a design block and tapping with the side of a round shaft.

10 Flux and set up the elements in position, using binding wire to hold them onto the band. (See Diagram C on page 32.) Solder the elements at the same time.

11 File, sand, and polish the overlays, edges, and inside of the ring. Slightly round the inner corner edges for comfort. Finish the outer surface with a medium plastic abrasive wheel. Polish the edges, using a hard felt wheel charged with rouge.

Torch Song Earrings

Photo by Ralph Gabriner

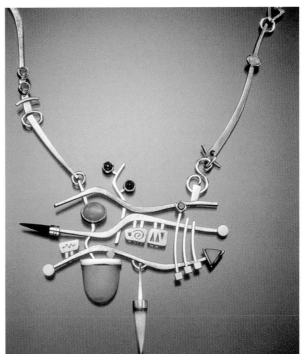

Tori Gates Necklace

Photo by Ralph Gabriner

SAM BROWN

Photo by Hap Sakwa

Gold Rings   *Gold Rings*

At the age of five, Sam Brown was already creating jewelry in the back of his Dad's electrical shop. Made out of scrap copper and brass, Sam's earliest work was motivated as much by his innate desire to create, as it was a chance to use all those neat tools his father had. Several decades later, Sam still makes jewelry and he is still motivated as much by the machinery and tools as he is by an ever-present need to be productive. When asked why he makes jewelry these days, Sam replies, "Making jewelry is my way of expressing the ideas in my head. And sometimes I design a piece just so I can justify buying a tool I have wanted for a while."

For many years, jewelry was only one of two full-time passions consuming Sam. He also devoted himself to rigorous daily equestrian training, with an eye on the Olympics. He honed his jewelry-making skills and, when not riding or studying, he created medieval-style jewelry. In order to see, firsthand, the medieval and gothic art and architecture he had read so much about, Sam took a vacation to Great Britain. On the trip he was fortunate to have met, Brian Clarke, an Irish master silversmith, who invited him to work in his studio. Returning home to California and armed with a bag of new skills, Sam became a specialist in Celtic-inspired jewelry. "Customers really liked what I was doing," Sam says. "Everyone could relate to the classical forms and by then I was able to make jewelry I was really proud of."

Sam enjoys the rich heritage of goldsmithing. He devotes a part of his time to teaching, as a way to stretch his own abilities, to understand better what he does, and to experience the excitement of learning through others.

These days, Sam has the freedom to come and go, to travel around the world, studying and gathering ideas. He is able to

SCB concentrate on satisfying the urge that lead to his early experimentation all those years ago.

"In my life, many interests have come and gone, but jewelry and metalsmithing are where my true love lies. I love each and every piece I make. I think that is something most people cannot say about their work."

Photo by Pamela Kramer

Photo by Hap Sakwa

Sam's 18k° gold, pearl and gem pendant is a timeless design with a classical motif. Its simple lines give it both traditional and contemporary appeal.

PEARL AND GEM PENDANT

Materials		Measurements
	Oval cabochon	18 mm x 13 mm
	Cultured pearl	7 mm
18k	Yellow gold round wire	2.5 mm diameter x 65 mm long
18k	Yellow gold sheet	0.5 mm (24 gauge) x 30 mm x 20 mm; 1 mm (18 gauge)
18k	Yellow gold square wire	0.8 mm x 10 mm

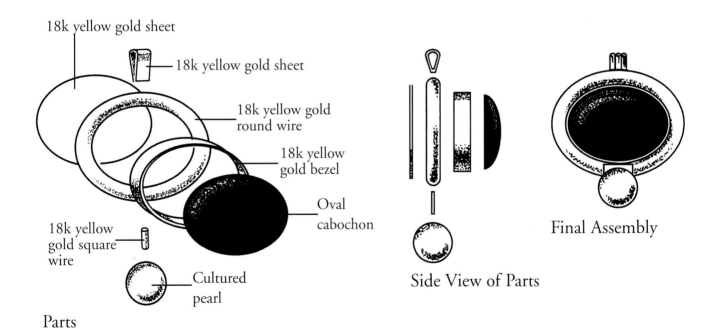

18k yellow gold sheet

18k yellow gold sheet

18k yellow gold round wire

18k yellow gold bezel

Oval cabochon

18k yellow gold square wire

Cultured pearl

Parts

Side View of Parts

Final Assembly

PEARL AND GEM PENDANT

1   Begin by making a bezel, 3 mm tall from 0.5 mm gold sheet for the cabochon. The length of the bezel can be determined by merely bending annealed gold round wire around the stone, marking, cutting, and soldering with gold hard solder.

2   Take the 2.5 mm gold round wire and make an oval border that fits around the outside of the bezel. Again, either the wrap-and-cut or the calculation method can be used (the outside of the bezel is used for calculations instead of the stone's dimensions.) Join the ends with hard solder.

Boulder Opal Pendants   Photo by Hap Sakwa

3   Add a quality stamp and maker's mark on the back of the 0.5 mm gold sheet to be used as the base. Place the bezel and ornamental border on the sheet, adjust to a perfect fit, and solder in place with medium solder. Cut around the border with a saw.

4   Trim or file the backing so the edges are not visible from the front. Taper the backing sheet so that it flows smoothly into the round wire border. If the stone is translucent, cut out the interior of the backing so that light can enter the stone from behind.

5   Cut a bail blank, 6 mm x 22 mm from 1 mm gold sheet. Form into a teardrop cross section. Solder the two ends, using gold hard solder. File two grooves and sand.

6   Use yellow ochre or another flow inhibitor, if necessary, to prevent prior seams of the same temperature solder from flowing. Place the bail in position against the rest of the piece and solder with gold medium solder.

7   Saw and file a square opening in the bottom of the pendant to accommodate the pearl. Drill a 0.8 mm hole in the top of the opening for the post. Taper the end, insert, and solder the 0.8 mm gold square wire post into place with gold easy solder. Twist the post to harden it and give a texture for the epoxy to hold onto inside the pearl. If necessary, enlarge the hole in the pearl to fit over the post. Cut the post to fit.

8   File, finish, and polish the piece.

9   Set the cabochon first, using either a bezel pusher or a hammer and punches. Use five-minute epoxy to glue the pearl onto the post.

DAVID CLARKSON

Photo by David Clarkson

"I love making jewelry," says David Clarkson. "I find it remarkable that after thirty years at this craft, I still wake up eager to go to work in the morning. And even after a long day, I often stay late to complete whatever it is I am working on."

In the late 60's, David took a job helping a production jeweler in Boston's hip Harvard Square district. Although it does not seem like much today, the $2 per hour he earned (less deductions) was enough for him to live on. David was quite content being paid to learn basic jewelry work in wire— bending, soldering, and forging. Even today, these techniques are the foundation of his work. "After a couple of years," David recalls, "a goldsmith friend and I left the frigid New England winters to strike out on our own in sunny California." The two formed a partnership and created a store/workshop on the California coast in a former dulcimer factory, where they used old fret boards as firewood. "Being out on my own," David says, "I learned quickly about making a living at jewelry. This included both design and craftsmanship. After all, my livelihood depended on it."

Although the partnership quickly fell apart, David stayed in the area and opened his own small store in a tiny coastal town with 200 residents. He later relocated the store and workshop to the picturesque town of Point Reyes Station, just north of San Francisco.

When he first put hammer to metal in 1968, David

Braided Rings

Photo by Ralph Gabriner

Cultured Pearl Earrings

Photo by Ralph Gabriner

had no clue that he was embarking on a career as an artisan in metal. But like his jewelry, he has forged and polished his skills day by day over the last quarter century. "I lead a good

life," David reflects. "I have a wife and daughter whom I love, a dog that does not talk back, and an outlet for my creativity that pays the bills. But above all," David says, "I have been able to bring happiness to a lot of people through jewelry that I made with my own hands. And that is a priceless reward."

FORGED BANGLE

Photo by Ralph Gabriner

Traditional in its creation, this forged silver bangle
is contemporary in its design with each hammer
blow by the maker adding to the appeal.

FORGED BANGLE

Materials	*Measurements*
Sterling silver round wire	4 mm

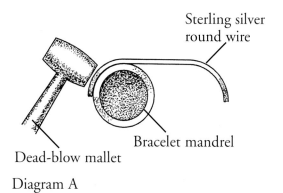

Sterling silver round wire

Bracelet mandrel

Dead-blow mallet

Diagram A

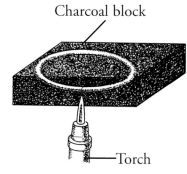

Charcoal block

Torch

Diagram B

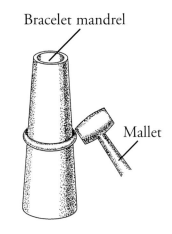

Bracelet mandrel

Mallet

Diagram C

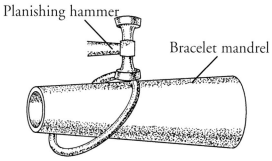

Planishing hammer

Bracelet mandrel

Diagram D

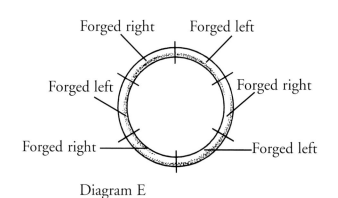

Forged right · Forged left

Forged left · Forged right

Forged right · Forged left

Diagram E

FORGED BANGLE

Ear Caressers

Photo by Ralph Gabriner

1 Use a saw to cut 170 cm (6¾") of 4 mm sterling silver wire for the bracelet, depending on the size of the wearer and the skill of the maker.

2 Bend the ends with pliers or with a dead-blow mallet around a highly polished bracelet mandrel. The material should look like a "C" with a straight middle section. (See Diagram A on page 40.)

3 Close the ends. It is not essential that the bracelet be round at this point, so long as the ends meet flush.

4 Place the bracelet on a charcoal block with the fluxed seam hanging over the edge. Add hard solder and heat an area around the seam. When the solder flows, draw it through the seam. Quench and pickle the bracelet, then rinse and dry. (See Diagram B on page 40.)

5 Place the bangle around the bracelet mandrel and use a mallet to force it up in size while rounding it. (See Diagram C on page 40.)

6 Polish the bracelet now to remove any scratches that would otherwise be hammered into the metal and to make the final polishing easier or even eliminate it entirely.

7 Divide the bangle into sixths indicated by a permanent marker.

8 With the bracelet around the mandrel and held at an angle of 30°, use a highly polished planishing hammer to strike the midpoint between two marks. Continue to hammer the metal with successively lighter blows moving outward towards the marks. Forging the metal like this will thin it most in the middle, tapering toward no alteration at the marks. With each hammer blow, the bangle increases in size. (See Diagram D on page 40.)

9 When the metal is partially forged, stop and move 120° further around the bracelet, and repeat the forging process, having skipped one section between two marks. Repeat again after rotating another 120°. (See Diagram E on page 40.)

10 Remove the bangle, flip it over and place it on the mandrel again. Repeat the process on the three untouched areas, forging them in the same way, but from the other side of the bracelet.

11 With all six faces started, check for continuity and continue to forge them thinner and wider until the metal is about 1.5 mm thick at the thinnest points in the middle of each section.

12 If the tools and metal were polished to begin with, the forged bracelet now has lots of reflective facets (hammer marks). If not, buff and polish as needed, although this will round the facets.

JEFF GEORGANTES

As a youngster filled with teenage angst in Lafayette, California, Jeff Georgantes was worried sick that he was never going to be good at anything. All of his friends it seemed, excelled at something; science, sports, petty crime, etc. Jeff felt left out until he took a high school crafts class. Much to his surprise, Jeff's cast blob-like silver ring turned out better than any of the other blob-like rings in the class. At last he had found something he excelled in and his life's path lay clearly ahead of him.

Jeff Georgantes

Jeff has come a long way since that first silver ring. He went on to receive a BA in Art and an MA in Sculpture from Humboldt State University in California. In addition, he has taken workshops at various locations around the country, including Haystack, Penland, Summer Vail, and the Revere Academy. When he reflects on the development of his work over the past twenty-five years, Jeff says, "In the beginning, I was influenced by a number of personal "heroes" in the jewelry/metalsmithing field. What I liked was the fact that these accomplished metalsmiths chose an approach that was playful, rather than the stiff formality seen in much of the jewelry world." Jeff preferred the work of those who displayed what he calls, "an irreverent reverence" for materials and subjects.

"I like to incorporate images and materials, which are not ordinarily considered precious, in a precious way," Jeff says. "I am very influenced by the natural environment where I live, juxtaposing precious materials like gold and silver with found beach shells, stones, and refuse from the age we live in." Much of Jeff's current work reflects his home on the Pacific Coast, 300 miles North of San Francisco. Jeff has also taught jewelry making at the college level, and he currently co-coordinates the Mendocino Art Center's (CA) Jewelry/Metalsmithing program.

Feeling Lucky Bola

Photo by Bob Pottberg

Photo by Bob Pottberg

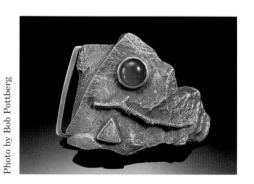

Photo by Bob Pottberg

Jeff's workshop is strewn with masses of raw materials, parts and pieces of this and that collected over the years. "I usually start with a central image and combine it with other materials until a concept says, 'Yes,' to me," explains the artist, "and then I am off and running."

42

Photo by Bob Pottberg

Jeff's recent series of antique bottle cap badges calls to mind an era when bottle caps were backed with cork. "As children we would pry the cork from of the back of bottle caps and then reinsert it after capturing a portion of a tee-shirt, to make a badge," Jeff recalls. "I remember how much fun it was to make a piece of jewelry with the cap from my favorite soda pop." Here is a way for us grown-ups to relive that personal connection with everyday objects that we found so captivating as children.

ALERT BOTTLE CAP BADGE

Materials		*Measurements*
	Sterling silver sheet	0.8 mm (20 gauge)
	Garnet cabochons	4 mm - 2 pieces
	Antique bottle cap	
	Fine silver bezel wire	0.3 mm (28 gauge) x 3 mm
	Sterling silver tubing	4 mm diameter; 5 mm diameter x 0.5 mm wall
14k	Yellow gold sheet	0.3 mm (28 gauge)
	Stainless steel ruler	
	Used pencil	
	Brass hexagonal bolts and nuts	4 sets with 1 mm shafts
	Stainless steel pin mechanism	
	Stainless steel wire	0.8 mm (20 gauge)
	Sterling silver round wire	2.6 mm (10 gauge)

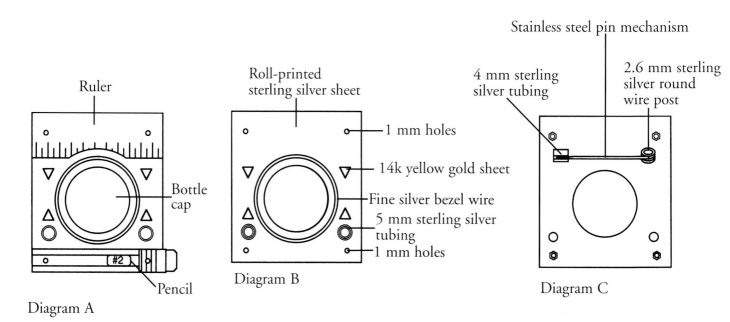

Diagram A

Ruler

Bottle cap

Pencil

Diagram B

Roll-printed sterling silver sheet

1 mm holes

14k yellow gold sheet

Fine silver bezel wire

5 mm sterling silver tubing

1 mm holes

Diagram C

Stainless steel pin mechanism

4 mm sterling silver tubing

2.6 mm sterling silver round wire post

ALERT BOTTLE CAP BADGE

1 Begin by rolling an annealed piece of 0.8 mm sterling silver sheet through the mill, against an etched brass plate to transfer the pattern. Anneal and flatten the silver. Trim to 45 mm x 50 mm. File and sand the edges.

2 From 5 mm sterling silver tubing, cut two pieces for the bezels. File the tops and bottoms flat, leaving 1.5 mm sections. Form fine silver bezel wire around the bottle cap. Cut and join the ends with silver hard solder.

Cherry Bottle Cap Badge

3 Cut the pencil and ruler to fit. Cut four 3 mm triangles from 0.3 mm gold sheet.

4 Place the bezels, triangles, pencil, and ruler in position on the back plate. Mark locations for the bolts, and drill four 1 mm holes through the back plate, pencil, and ruler. (See Diagram A on page 44.)

5 Solder three bezels and four triangles in position on the plate with silver medium solder. Pickle and rinse. Drill a 1 mm starter hole inside the bezels. (See Diagram B on page 44.)

6 Prepare a 5 mm section of 4 mm sterling silver tubing for the tube catch. Solder to the back of the pin with silver easy solder. With a saw, slit the tubing lengthwise below center, to accept the pin stem. Solder a 2.6 mm sterling silver round wire post, 5 mm tall, onto the back with silver easy solder. Drill a 0.8 mm hole through the post for the pin stem. (See Diagram C on page 44.)

Gone Fishin' Brooch

7 Oxidize the back plate with liver-of-sulfur and rub the highlights with an abrasive pad. Polish the triangles with a felt wheel mounted in a flex shaft.

8 Set the stones with a hammer and punch. Set the bottle cap with a burnisher.

9 Bolt the pencil and ruler in place and use a drop of five-minute epoxy to lock the nuts.

10 Insert the end of the 0.8 mm stainless steel wire into the hole in the post. Wrap the wire around a few times to secure, then cut. File a taper and line it up with the tube catch. Adjust so that the tension holds the sharpened end of the pin stem in the catch. Sign the piece on the back with a vibro-engraver.

IRA SHERMAN

Photo by Bob Goldman

Inventor of mechanical sculpture; creator of sterling silver Judaica; restorer of architectural metalwork; designer of elegant jewelry. All of these descriptions fit Ira Sherman. A native of Chicago, Ira originally studied biology and chemistry. However, those staid disciplines didn't satisfy the artist waiting inside his complex mind. Bored by formal education, Ira recalls, "I sought refuge from the rigidity of science in the sculpture studio." Although he never abandoned his intrigue with math, mechanics, and science, Ira's interest in art continued to grow and sculpture became his medium for self-expression.

In the years following college, Ira devoted himself to building his metalsmithing skills. "The knowledge and techniques used to manipulate metal have had powerful mythical and magical connotations throughout history," says the artist. "I chose metal as my medium because of its limitless mechanical, ductile, structural and aesthetic qualities." Working primarily in jewelry, Ira won a series of awards early in his career and he quickly earned the respect of his peers. Ira continues to make jewelry although he has branched out into allied areas, such as religious metalwork and large sculpture. Ira uses jewelry as a testing ground to develop seed concepts for larger pieces. Some become monumental sculptures while others evolve into his unique collection of body-hugging mechanical devices.

In addition to his jewelry and mechanicals, Ira produces Judaica, liturgical items for Jewish observance, such as candleholders and wine cups. Ira also consults for and runs a small business reconstructing architectural metalwork for older buildings.

It would seem that going in different directions at the same time would be confusing and overwhelming. In fact the opposite is true. "While working in four seemingly unrelated metal disciplines, jewelry, interactive sculpture, architectural metalwork, and liturgical silversmithing," explains the artist, "I find each enhances and influences the other." Jewelry remains the most important medium for Ira. In jewelry he can pursue lyrical design and experiment with aesthetics. "Jewelry is my prime resource when I need ideas for large, more monumental work," he says.

Stepping back for a moment, Ira confesses that, "Given a life free of all responsibilities, I would disappear into my studio and create working sculptural appliances to change the world!"

Gold Mesh Bracelet

Photo by Ira Sherman

FORGED AND CAST MESH PIN

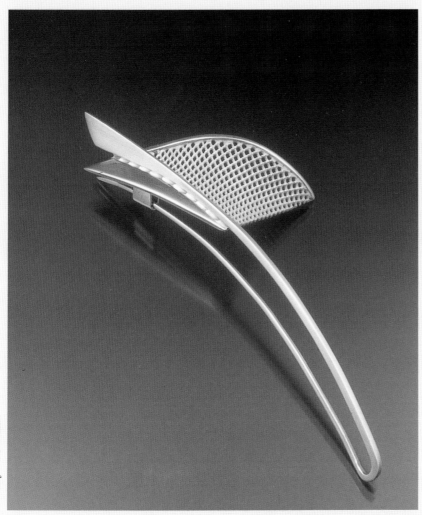

Photo by Ira Sherman

This pin is composed of two distinct design elements which are made separately and then joined together. One is a sleek forged white gold needle. The other is a textural section of yellow gold mesh, cast from the plastic netting used to hold vegetables. The two components contrast sharply in color, texture, placement, shape, and function.

FORGED AND CAST MESH PIN

Materials		*Measurements*
14k	Yellow gold casting shot	
14k	Yellow gold round wire	1.3 mm diameter (16 gauge)
14k	White gold rod	2.6 mm (10 gauge)

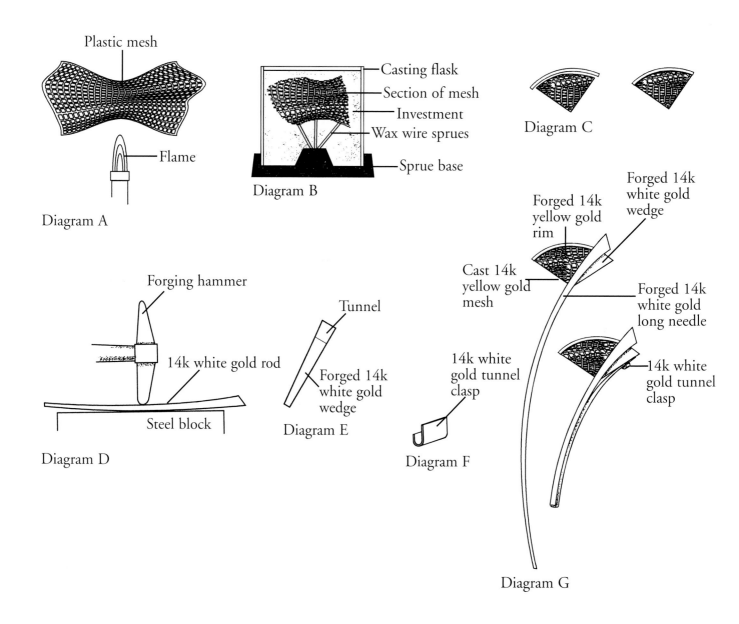

Diagram A — Plastic mesh / Flame

Diagram B — Casting flask / Section of mesh / Investment / Wax wire sprues / Sprue base

Diagram C

Diagram D — Forging hammer / 14k white gold rod / Steel block

Diagram E — Tunnel / Forged 14k white gold wedge

Diagram F — 14k white gold tunnel clasp

Diagram G — Forged 14k yellow gold rim / Forged 14k white gold wedge / Cast 14k yellow gold mesh / Forged 14k white gold long needle / 14k white gold tunnel clasp

FORGED AND CAST MESH PIN

1   Take a piece of plastic grocery mesh and slowly warm it over an open flame until the plastic begins to shrink. This material gets hot enough to burn your skin so either wear gloves or be certain not to overheat it. (See Diagram A on page 48.) While the mesh is still hot, form it to the shape you want and hold it in that position as it cools. Use scissors to cut the desired section from the larger piece.

2   On a commercial rubber sprue base, attach several wax wire "sprues" which will act as pipelines for molten gold during casting. Attach the sprues to the edges of the mesh. More sprues increase the likelihood of a complete casting. The only disadvantage of overspruing is the extra work cutting them off later. Otherwise the more sprues, the better. Slide a casting flask over the model so that it sits firmly within the sprue base. Mix a batch of investment (a special refractory, plaster-like substance). Pour the investment into the flask, covering the model. Allow to cure for several hours. Remove the rubber sprue base. (See Diagram B on page 48.)

Gold Mesh Pin

Photo by Ira Sherman

3   Place the flask in the burnout oven with the opening down and heat. The wax and plastic will melt out and then vaporize, leaving a hollow cavity. Prepare to cast the form in 14k yellow gold in a centrifuge. Since there is a lot of detail, it will take the metal an extra instant to flow throughout the mesh. Therefore overheat the metal a bit more than usual prior to casting. Cast the mesh model.

4   After casting, remove the gold mesh model, cut off the sprues, and file the edges. Finish and polish the gold mesh element.

5   Form the 1.3 mm round wire into a rim for the edge of the mesh, leaving the ends longer than necessary. Use binding wire to hold the pieces in position and solder them together with 14k yellow gold hard solder. Then trim the ends of the wire rim flush with the mesh. (See Diagram C on page 48.)

6   For the main white gold element, cut off about 75 mm of the 2.6 mm rod and, with a forging hammer, shape one end to a long tapered needle. Forge the other end out flat, to a thickness of about 1 mm. (See Diagram D on page 48.) Use a planishing hammer with a slightly domed face to "planish" (flatten) the surface, removing the marks left by forging.

7   Use another 25 mm of the white gold rod to forge a piece similar to the flattened end of the long element, but without the needle. From this piece, cut off the end which should be about 0.6 mm thick. This will become the tunnel clasp. (See Diagram E on page 48.)

8   Anneal and form this piece into a "U" for the "tunnel" clasp. Adjust it so that one side is about 1.5 mm longer than the other. The longer side will be soldered and the smaller side will permit the needle to enter. (See Diagram F on page 48.)

9   File, sand, and polish the white gold components. Determine the exact position of the two forged elements against the mesh. Flux and flow 14k yellow gold medium solder onto the forged pieces, where contact will be made. Pickle, rinse, and dry. Cover most of the mesh with typewriter correction fluid, leaving the areas to be joined with the forged elements bare. *Note: Take appropriate precautions against inhalation.* Allow the fluid to dry. The only exposed metal should be exactly where the two forged elements will touch the mesh. Flux the exposed areas of the mesh and the contact points on the forged elements.

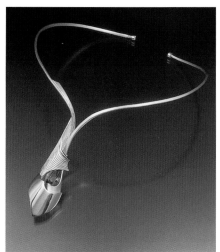

Neckpiece with Rhodalite Garnet

Photo by Ira Sherman

10 Use binding wire, steel wire support jigs, pieces of charcoal, etc., to arrange the elements on a soldering block in such a way that they meet properly. *Note: Solder flows toward the heat and also with gravity, so you should set up and heat accordingly.* Solder the pieces together by heating them and drawing the solder from the forged elements to the mesh. Do not quench white gold. When the assembly is air cooled, pickle, rinse, and dry the metal.

11 Use correction fluid to block out all areas of the pieces except where the clasp will sit, behind the smaller forged element. Position and solder the tunnel with 14k white gold easy solder along the long side. Pickle, rinse, and dry.

12 Most of the larger element should still be hard from forging because of its distance from the heat of soldering. Fold the needle and forge it further to harden it at the bend. Adjust the length to slide into the open side of the tunnel. Adjust the tension so that the needle actually snaps into place. (See Diagram G on page 48.)

13 Apply a final polish as needed.

RICHARD MESSINA

"As long as I can remember, I have been an artist." Richard Messina says. Born in Italy, Richard feels a strong kinship with the Italian tradition of fine arts, sculpture, and goldsmithing. When he was ten years old, Richard's parents took him to New York City where he first saw the work of Scandinavian silversmith, Georg Jenson, as well as Brancusi's famous sculpture, "Bird in Space." Both have been major influences of Messina's work ever since.

At around the same time that he discovered motorcycling, Richard learned to work in precious metals from his father, who was a dentist. His two passions, motorcycles and jewelry, both rely on engineering, metallurgy, metalsmithing, fitting the human form, and, of course, fine design to perform their functions well. His father taught Richard to work in wax, creating models that he then cast into gold and silver. Since the process of lost-wax casting for jewelry and dentistry are virtually identical, he applied his newly acquired skills to making jewelry. At first his work went to family and friends, and then a following developed and grew to the point where he supported himself exclusively with his work. Combining a natural gift with the perfect training, Richard became very proficient in making jewelry and small sculpture. And despite the fact that he was primarily self-taught, his talents lead to a teaching post at Parsons School of Design in New York.

Although a master of casting, Richard then set his sights on the other major way in which jewelers work—forging metal directly with hammers. Forging and forming require tremendous skill to control the metal, but the results are worth the effort. "Unlike casting, where metal is weak and lacks structural integrity," explains Richard, "forging compacts and hardens the metal, which makes it springier and stronger." For this reason, the metal feels more solid. With a belief that metalsmiths must be artists as well as engineers in order to work effectively, Richard creates jewelry which clearly displays his devotion to both disciplines. Ever the aesthete, Richard also appreciates the engineering in what he rides, "My motorcycle is a combination of functional sculpture and machine rolled into one." Like his jewelry, his motorcycle reinforces his strong belief that form follows function.

Photo by Ann Dunn

Forged Torque and Cuff

Photo by Ralph Gabriner

FORGED GOLD FIBULA WITH A CULTURED PEARL

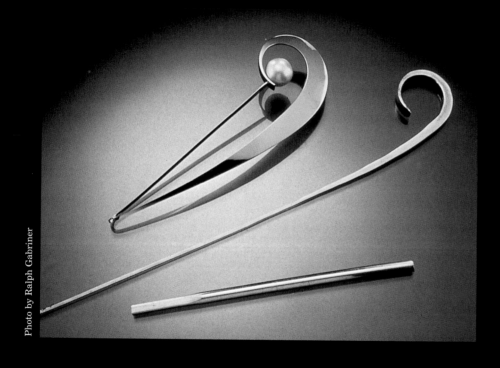

Photo by Ralph Gabriner

Based on the classical garment clasp, this gold fibula is as modern as tomorrow. It combines graceful lines with the strength and integrity of cold-forged gold.

FORGED GOLD FIBULA WITH A CULTURED PEARL

Materials		*Measurements*
14k	Yellow gold rod	2.5 mm (10 gauge) diameter x 7.6 cm (3") long
14k	Yellow gold tubing	2 mm outside diameter x 0.5 mm wall
	Cultured pearl	8 mm

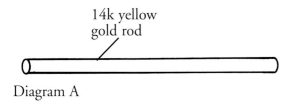

14k yellow
gold rod

Diagram A

Diagram B

Diagram C

Diagram D

Diagram E

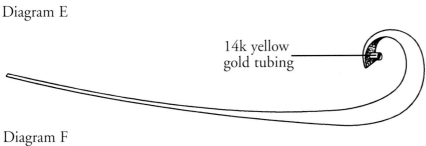

14k yellow
gold tubing

Diagram F

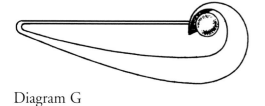

Diagram G

Photo by Ralph Gabriner

Hoop Earrings

FORGED GOLD FIBULA WITH A CULTURED PEARL

1   Anneal the gold rod, if it is not already soft. (See Diagram A on page 53.)

2   To create an even taper, the metal is step-rolled in the mill. To do this, insert the rod into the wire portion of the mill, finding a setting where the metal barely makes contact so that it will not slide between the rollers. Close the rolls, or if they are already closed, move down to the next smaller opening and adjust the rolls to make contact. Roll the rod into the mill, about ⅔ of its length. Stop and roll the rod back out. Close the rollers a bit and roll the bar in again, without rotating it. Repeat this sequence of rolling in, rolling out, each time closing the rolls and inserting the metal a little bit less to create the steps. Stop when there are several steps tapering down from the original size to a section that is 1 mm x 1 mm for 70 mm. This will become the pin stem. (See Diagram B on page 53.) Do not anneal the metal because you want it to be very hard and springy. Trim the flashing of metal that has squeezed out the sides of the rollers.

3   Use a 20 ounce forging hammer over a large steel block or anvil to remove the steps. Many well-directed blows result in a piece that has a continuous taper with a square cross section. (See Diagram C on page 53.)

4   Forge only the thick end of the rod flat and flare it, using a polished cross peen hammer. At this point, the wide end is about 5 mm x 0.6 mm. (See Diagram D on page 53.)

5   Using a round mandrel and a nylon mallet, shape the flattened end of the metal to generate the initial curve of the fibula. (See Diagram E on page 53.)

6 Use a forging hammer to flatten the curved portion which still has a square cross section, just within the flattened end of the fibula. Forge this in a plane across that of the end. Precisely placed flat hammer blows control the curve and spread of the gold. Blows that are slightly tilted toward the outside of the curve will decrease the radius of the curve. In other words, if you want the metal to curve to the left, hit it with the hammer canted a few degrees to the right of perpendicular, so that the outside of the curve thins and gets longer. (See Diagram F on page 53.)

Leaves

Photo by Ralph Gabriner

7 Take the piece directly from the anvil to a specialized polishing unit, called a split lap machine, which is ideal for finishing and polishing flat surfaces. Use a "flint hard" lap wheel charged with tripoli to true the curves and correct the planes. The final "optical" finish is created on a standard polishing lathe, using a knife-edge buff charged with red rouge.

Photo by Ralph Gabriner

8 Solder a 5 mm section of gold tubing to the flattened end of the curve, in a position so that the pearl will look nestled in the crook of the curve. Use a 1 mm bit to drill through the tube and the fibula where the tube is attached to create the catch of the pin mechanism. (See Diagram G on page 54.)

Channel Cuff

Photo by Ralph Gabriner

Sails

9 Bend the long tapered end at the point where the sharpened end will pass through the hole and about 2 mm into the tube. File the pin to a round cross section, sand and polish it, then use the split lap to shape the tip of the wire to a blunt point.

10 Drill an 8 mm pearl with a 2 mm bit so that it just slides over the tube. Cement the pearl in place.

MICHAEL SUGARMAN

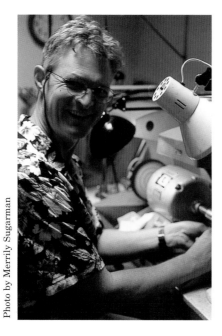

Photo by Merrily Sugarman

"Rapidly approaching my fiftieth birthday, I find myself questioning things that I had previously taken for granted," Michael Sugarman said recently. "I have been a goldsmith and designer for half my life and I suppose it would be fair to say that I am just a maker of 'trinkets.' On the surface that sounds pretty trite, but I can honestly say that every piece of jewelry I have ever made has been an attempt to bring visual poetry into the world."

Growing up in suburban Northern California, Michael spent his youth listening to the Beach Boys, Jan and Dean, and the Beatles. After high school, Michael entered "the real world" by performing in a rock and roll band. A few years into his professional music career, he came to the conclusion that earning a livelihood by strumming a guitar was "iffy at best." In order to augment his irregular income, Michael took the first job he could, which was as low man on the totem pole for a small jewelry manufacturer. "All I did at first was file, sand, and polish metal—and I loved it," he recalls.

When some friends admired a piece he made for himself in off-hours, Michael realized that there might actually be a future for him in jewelry. So he sat down and made a few more pieces and took them to every store he could find that sold jewelry. The first potential customer he called on was a Rexal Drug store. By the end of the day he had made his first sale, $15 for a dozen pairs of forged silver earrings. Michael was off and running.

Hollow "J" Earrings

Photo by Ralph Gabriner

From that day onward, Michael worked full-time, making a living at jewelry. Over the years, he has established himself as an innovative designer/manufacturer on the national jewelry scene. He exhibits at the major jewelry trade events and sells his work exclusively through galleries and jewelry stores nationwide.

"What I like about making jewelry is the combination of engineering, invention, function and beauty," says the artist. "It challenges all of my abilities and enables me to express myself artistically, and at the same time, to make a living." But the real truth comes out as the child in Michael explains, "Making jewelry is like playing professional baseball. I'm a grown-up, getting paid to play my favorite game."

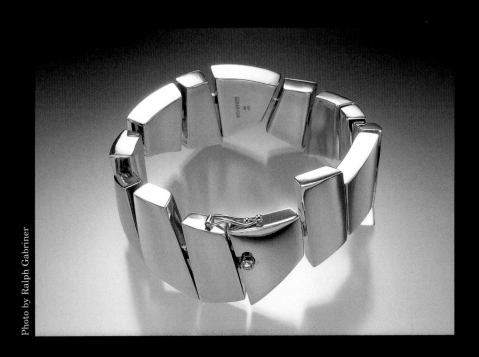

Photo by Ralph Gabriner

Inspired by a stone wall Michael constructed, this bracelet is composed of 13 individual "boxes." Each has four separate pieces of gold, with one small diamond used as a button to release the clasp. When complete, it rests on the wrist with a sensual yet architectonic simplicity.

BOULDER BRACELET

Materials   Measurements

Materials		Measurements
14k	White gold sheet (nickel alloy)	0.5 mm (24 gauge)
14k	Yellow gold sheet	1.3 mm (16 gauge); 0.5 mm (24 gauge), fully annealed
14k	Yellow gold tubing	3.3 mm outside diameter x 0.5 mm wall; 2 mm outside diameter x 0.5 mm wall
14k	Yellow gold round wire	1.0 mm (18 gauge)
	One diamond	0.07 carat (2.7 mm)

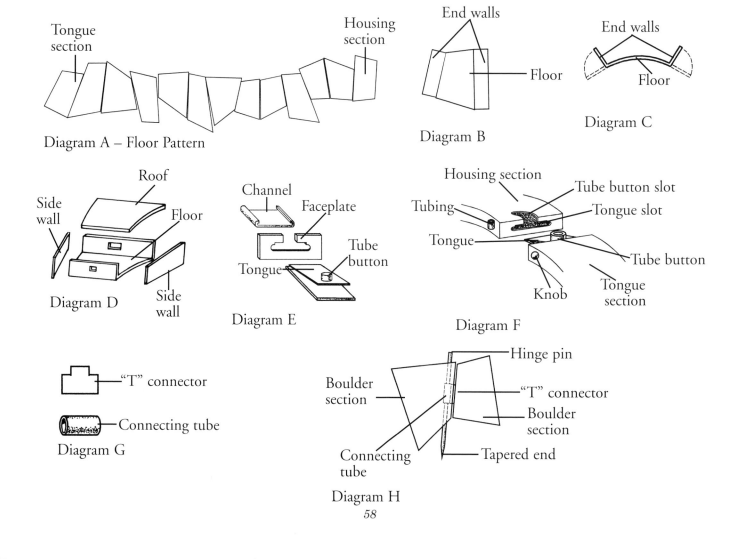

Tongue section   Housing section

Diagram A – Floor Pattern

End walls   Floor

Diagram B

End walls   Floor

Diagram C

Roof   Side wall   Floor   Side wall

Diagram D

Channel   Faceplate   Tube button   Tongue

Diagram E

Housing section   Tube button slot   Tongue slot   Tubing   Tongue   Tube button   Knob   Tongue section

Diagram F

"T" connector

Connecting tube

Diagram G

Hinge pin   Boulder section   "T" connector   Boulder section   Connecting tube   Tapered end

Diagram H

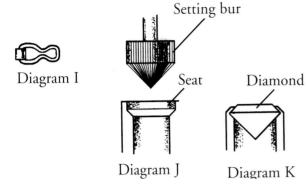

Setting bur

Diagram I

Seat

Diamond

Diagram J   Diagram K

Platinum Multiwire Band

Photo by Ralph Gabriner

BOULDER BRACELET

1 Sketch 13 four-sided boulder sections of the bracelet from the top view. (See Diagram A – Floor Pattern on page 58.) Copy each section that represents the floor pattern. Add the two end walls, 5 mm wide. (See Diagram B on page 58.) Transfer the sketches to 0.5 mm yellow gold sheet. Use a jeweler's saw to pierce out the 13 patterns. Use a sharp chisel-shaped punch to make indentations on the fold lines between the floor and walls. Shape the pieces to follow a gentle curve of a wrist by using a mallet to form them against a bracelet mandrel. Fold up the walls, along the creases to 90°. (See Diagram C on page 58.)

2 Layout the folded boulder sections in sequence, with a tongue section on the left and a housing section (to receive the tongue) on the right. (See Diagram A on page 58.) On the left end wall of all sections, except the tongue section, layout, pierce, and file a rectangular hole, 1.3 mm x 2 mm. On the right end wall of all sections, except the housing section, layout, pierce, and file a larger rectangular

hole 4 mm x 2 mm. (See Diagram D on page 58.) Remove the right end wall on the housing section.

3 Prepare tongue from a 22 mm long strip of 0.5 mm white gold sheet. It should be 10 mm wide for 12 mm length, stepping down to 8 mm wide for the remaining 10 mm in its length. (See Diagram E on page 58.)

4 Make a channel 10 mm wide and 24 mm long to receive the tongue from an annealed piece of 0.5 yellow gold sheet. Center the 10 mm wide section of the tongue across the channel strip, which is then tightly folded up and around the tongue so that the ends almost meet at the top of the channel. Trim the folded ends back, leaving an opening 8 mm wide at the top of the channel. (See Diagram E on page 58.)

5 Without scoring, fold the tongue strip at the step and press the fold completely flat. The 10 mm wide bottom of the tongue should slide smoothly in the channel with the 8 mm wide top in the space between the folded edges of the channel.

Photo by Ralph Gabriner

Pavé Solitaire Ring

6 Carve a slot for the channel into a piece of 0.5 mm yellow gold sheet that will become the end wall and faceplate on the housing section. (See Diagram E on page 58.) Insert the end of the channel into the slot and solder them together with yellow gold hard solder. Trim the excess of the channel flush with the front of the faceplate. Above the opening in the channel and flush with the edges, carve a space 8 mm wide x 0.5 mm tall. Test the fit by inserting the tongue. The tongue should slide smoothly into the channel and when fully inserted, the top snaps up behind the faceplate. Use a poker to push it down and withdraw the tongue. Adjust until it works smoothly. Centered above the channel, cut a 3.5 mm wide vertical slot in the faceplate for the tube button. Solder the faceplate in position on the right end of the housing section. Trim the excess. Check the fit of the tongue. Carve a 0.5 mm tall x 10 mm wide slot for the protruding bottom tab of the tongue into the left end of the tongue section.

7 Solder a 4 mm tall section of 3.3 mm yellow gold tubing onto the tongue with yellow hard solder for the tube button. Tubing should be flush with the end of the tongue, centered left to right.

8 File the side edges of all boulder sections flat. Place each unit on its side on 0.5 mm yellow gold sheet and scribe the sidewalls. (See Diagram D on page 58.) Use a saw and cut out a bit oversized. Use binding wire to hold the pieces together and join with yellow gold hard solder. Do not clean up the excess until later. File the top edges flush, with a curve that matches the floor.

9 Cut out 13 roof sections on the 0.5 mm yellow gold sheet and form them to match the contour of each floor. (See Diagram D on page 58.) Bind and join with yellow gold hard solder. File all edges flush; sand with medium and then fine abrasive paper.

10 Use a saw and file to carve a slot for the tube button in the roof of the housing section above the 3.5 mm wide slot in the faceplate. (See Diagram F on page 58.) It should be as deep as necessary to allow the top of the tongue to snap inside.

11 Insert the tongue into the housing, and the bottom tab into the tongue section. Mark the depth on the tab. Remove the tongue from the housing and solder it with easy solder into the small slot in the tongue section.

12 Make the "T" connector patterns on 1.3 mm yellow gold sheet. (See Diagram G on page 58.) Each small end is 2 mm wide and 1 mm long;

Tourmaline Constructed Ring

Photo by Ralph Gabriner

60

each large end is 4 mm wide and 2 mm long. Cut out and clean up the edges with a file. Attach a section of 2 mm gold tubing along the top of each "T", using yellow gold hard solder.

13 Test the fit of the small end of each connector into the small rectangular hole in the left end wall of each box. Fit should be tight. Adjust to fit and insert. Join the parts with yellow medium solder. (See Diagram H on page 58.)

14 Finely sand all surfaces of all sections. Remove the dust and use a cutting compound to buff them. Clean the sections and polish to a high luster.

15 Set a pair of dividers at 3 mm and make a small nick on both sidewalls adjacent to the large rectangular opening in each end wall. These mark the centers of the connecting tubes when the "T's" are inserted. Drill a 1 mm hole on each nick, centered between the roof and the floor. Remove the flashing. Create a very slight chamfer on both sides.

Hollow Sweep Earrings

16 Cut 12 straight pieces of 1 mm gold round wire for the hinge pins, each piece longer than required and tapered on one end. Insert the tube of one section into the large slot of the next. Correct the fit as necessary. Feed the tapered end of the pin through the hole in the wall, then through the connecting tube and out the other hole. (See Diagram H on page 58.) Repeat until all sections are temporarily attached.

17 Firecoat the entire assembly and solder all of the ends, using yellow gold easy solder. Do not pickle the assembly. Instead, immerse the assembly in boiling water. Clip, file, and sand the ends of the pins so they are flush with the side walls. When polished, they become invisible.

18 Solder a 2 mm section of 2 mm gold tubing to one side of the housing section, 3 mm from the end. (See Diagram F on page 58.) Use yellow gold easy solder, being cautious not to melt other seams. Solder a 2 mm spherical knob, created by fusing up a ball of gold, onto the tongue section. (See Diagram F on page 58.) With the tongue in the housing, insert a 1 mm piece of gold round wire into the tubing, creating the safety. Fold into "U", then bring ends together, allowing it to fit over the knob. Adjust; solder the ends of the "U" together. (See Diagram I on page 59.) Readjust for a tight fit, evidenced by an audible click.

19 Cut the button tube down so that when the clasp is closed it sticks out 2 mm. Use a setting bur the same size as the diamond to cut a seat. (See Diagram J on page 59.) Insert the stone, then close over the "bezel" with a pusher. (See Diagram K on page 59.) Clean up the edge with gentle abrasive wheels. Buff and polish the setting.

Photo by Ra;ph Gabriner

DEE FONTANS

Photo by Charles Lewton-Brain

Girls Without Shirts

Photo by Charles Lewton-Brain

The thread that ties Dee Fontans' work together is her fascination with the female form. She began her formal art training by meticulously copying the paintings of masters, and then continued at the Parson School of Design in New York. Her interest in drawing the human figure lead to a major in jewelry design for which she received a BFA with honors at SUNY New Paltz.

In addition to cloisonné and other enameling techniques, Dee uses what is known as the "grisaille" technique to build her figures in layers of white on a black background. This enables Dee to capture each pose fully in three dimensions. Grisaille rests at the confluence of her dual training as a figure artist/painter and as a metalsmith/jeweler. "The longevity of the material, its preciousness, the color and surface potential of enamel, as well as the technical expertise that is required, all draw me to this medium," explains the artist. "But best of all, grisaille offers me the means to convey depth and dimension not possible in any other medium."

But Dee's work goes beyond conventional personal adornment. She explains, "I see the whole form as a canvas. I don't limit myself within conventional boundaries by just creating jewelry in precious metals. My designs speak about changing the view of what beauty and age are in cultural terms.

Fontans has been a member of the faculty in the Jewelry/Metals program at Alberta College of Art and Design for the past eight years. In 1991, together with her husband Charles Lewton-Brain, she founded The Centre for Jewelry Studies in Calgary, Alberta, Canada. In addition to teaching in Calgary, Dee gives workshops across the US, Canada and in the Caribbean.

Dee's artistry stems from diverse cultures in her family tree. She integrates her heritage to explore the definitions of jewelry as body adornment, using both metal and textile jewelry. Not to be omitted is Dee's third inherited trait, passion, which she attributes to her father's ancestry. "Believing nothing happens in isolation," says Dee, "I am fascinated by the interrelationships around us. Art is about the connection between itself and the audience. Taken one step further, fashion and jewelry include the wearer, who gives life to body adornment, transforming it into a work of art."

A WOMAN OF COLOR; PRIMARIES: BLUE

"This piece was prompted by an invitation to design eyeglasses for a gallery exhibition. I made enameled eye cups with gold foil, chain, and weights over the ears to hold them in place. The series includes four pairs in different colors, each conveying a different emotion."

Photo by Charles Lewton-Brain

A WOMAN OF COLOR; PRIMARIES: BLUE

Materials		Measurements
	Copper sheet	0.6 mm (22 gauge); 1 mm (18 gauge)
	Brass wire	1 mm (18 gauge)
24k	Gold foil for enamel	
	Blue enamel powder	150 mesh
	Klyr-fire®	
	Gold-plated chain	

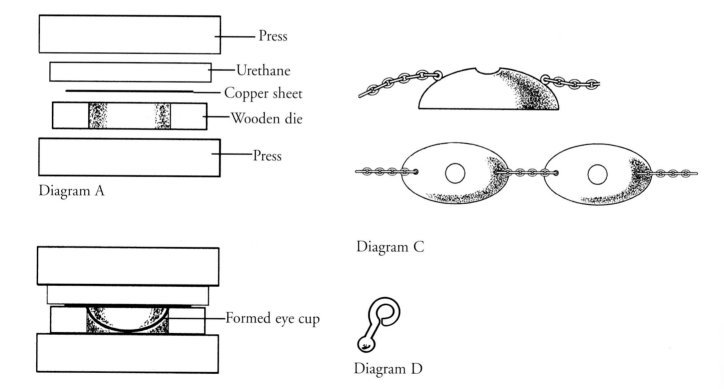

Diagram A

Diagram B

Diagram C

Diagram D

1 Cut a 25 mm x 45 mm oval hole in a piece of 14 mm thick wood to serve as silhouette die for the eye cups. (See Diagram A on page 64.)

2 Into a press or heavy vise, insert a sheet of annealed 0.6 mm copper, sandwiched between urethane and the wooden die.

3 Press two pieces of 0.6 mm copper sheet into the die for the two eye cups. Remove the metal and repeat until the forms are 13 mm deep. (See Diagram B on page 64.)

4 Saw around the oval perimeter of each cup and file the edges. Saw out two 20 mm circles from 1 mm copper sheet for the weights.

5 Layout 8 mm eye hole in the center of each cup. Drill a 1 mm starter hole in each and use a saw to pierce the eye holes. Drill 1.2 mm holes for the chain sections, 5 mm in from both sides of each eye cup. Drill 1.2 mm hole near the edge of each ear weight. (See Diagram C on page 64.)

6 Apply gum tragacanth to the insides of the cups and to one side of each weight. Sift blue enamel onto the surfaces. Place the work on trivets that support it by the edges only. Fire in the kiln to flow the enamel, remove and cool slowly. Repeat.

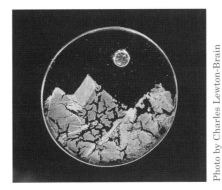

Moon Over the Mountain

Photo by Charles Lewton-Brain

7 Gently file to clean the edges, including the drilled holes, of the enameled components after each firing. Remove oxides from the unenameled surfaces by pickling after each firing.

8 Apply gum tragacanth to the outside of the cups as well as to the unenameled sides of the weights. Sift blue enamel onto the surfaces and fire. Clean and repeat.

9 Wet the outsides of the cups and one side of the weights. Use fine tweezers or a #000 sable brush to pick up small pieces of 24k gold foil. Arrange them on the enameled outside surfaces and to one side of the weights. Fire again, intentionally overheating the enamels to create a crackle effect.

Photo by Jay Robinson

A Woman of Color; Primaries: Red

10 File and sand the edges of components. Buff with tripoli and polish with rouge.

11 With a torch, ball up the ends of six segments of 1 mm brass wire for chain connectors. Use a pair of round-nose pliers to form loops in the ends. (See Diagram D on page 64.)

12 Cut three sections of chain: one approximately 50 mm to connect the cups across the bridge of the nose (depending on the wearer's anatomy), and two approximately 27 cm long for the ear weights. Insert the connectors from the inside of the cups. Insert the chain ends and close the loops. Use the last two connectors to attach the ear weights.

Photo by Charles Lewton-Brain

Cape May

Photo by Charles Lewton-Brain

Diane

ETIENNE PERRET

Photo by Mark Haskell

"I have always loved to make things with my hands," says Etienne Perret, recalling his youth in Switzerland and New York. "As a child, it was just trinkets and gadgets, and by high school, I was making jewelry for friends." While still in his teens, he opened a jewelry store in the coastal village of Camden, Maine. A very energetic and industrious man, Etienne has never stopped to look back.

The store proved successful; but a few years into it, Etienne decided he was not learning fast enough on his own. While maintaining the store, he enrolled at the Rhode Island School of Design, 250 miles away. For four years he commuted between the two. Graduating with a BFA, a better understanding of jewelry making, and a well-honed sense of design, Etienne looked to expanded horizons for his work. He began manufacturing and selling his jewelry to other stores through trade shows in New York, Basel, and Tokyo.

Ever in the forefront of jewelry design, Etienne has won international acclaim for his work, including three Diamonds Today Awards. Etienne's work often pushes the limits of what one thinks of as conventional jewelry. One of his designs includes a pair of ladies' stockings with 25 carats of diamonds glittering down the seam. Although it did not win an award, this outrageous piece of jewelry was featured on Lifestyles of the Rich and Famous and the Johnny Carson Show.

Reflecting on his lot, Etienne says, "I consider myself uncommonly fortunate to be able to design jewelry that is meaningful to me, using the best materials and craftsmanship. I get to travel to the glamour spots of the world, I have a family, and I live on the beautiful Maine Coast. I do not go to work, I just live my life."

Photo by Ralph Gabriner

Charm Collector's Necklace

Photo by Ralph Gabriner

Charm Bracelet

SPINNING LENTIL RING

This creation is based on Egyptian scarab rings
made thousands of years ago.

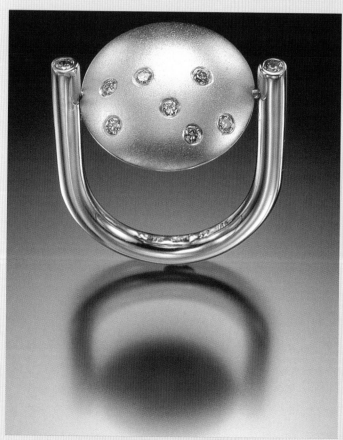

Photo by Ralph Gabriner

SPINNING LENTIL RING

Materials		Measurements
18k	Yellow gold wire	3 mm (approximately 9 gauge)
18k	Yellow gold sheet	0.65 mm (26 gauge)
950	Platinum sheet	0.65 mm (26 gauge)
950	Platinum wire	0.8 mm (24 gauge)
	Diamonds	0.04 carat (2.2 mm diameter) - 2 pieces
	Diamonds	0.01 to 0.02 carats (1.3 to 1.7 mm diameter) - several pieces

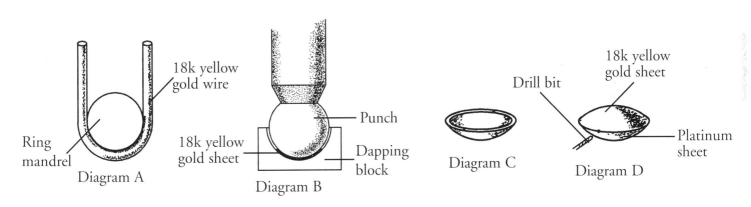

Diagram A

Diagram B

Diagram C

Diagram D

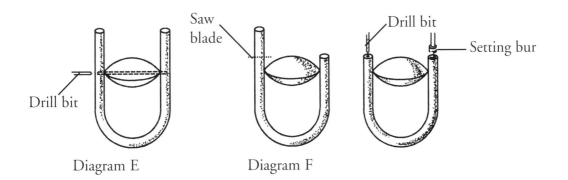

Diagram E

Diagram F

SPINNING LENTIL RING

1 Anneal an 80 mm section of 3 mm gold wire and form it around a ring mandrel into a "U", leaving an 18 mm space between the ends. (See Diagram A on page 69.)

2 Saw two discs from the gold and platinum sheets, 19 mm in diameter. Dome the discs with a 25 mm dapping punch in either a 27 mm concavity in a dapping block, or into a block of wood with a rounded depression. The discs should have a 4–4.5 mm depth when complete. (See Diagram B on page 69.)

3 File the edges of the discs with a flat file to ensure that they meet flush. File two small notches opposite each other on the edge of each disc. (See Diagram C on page 69.)

Starlight Wedding Bands

Rim Ring and Earrings

Photo by Ralph Gabriner

Photo by Ralph Gabriner

4 Match up the notches and join the discs together with 18k yellow gold hard solder. The lentil form should be 18 mm in diameter and 8–9 mm thick. (See Diagram D on page 69.)

5 Use a 0.8 mm drill to create small holes at the notches.

6 Polish both the lentil and the ring shank. Mark the ring with a quality stamp and maker's mark.

7 Position the lentil between the vertical posts of the shank so that the size is comfortable. Mark the hinge holes in the shank and drill with the same 0.8 mm twist drill. (See Diagram E on page 69.)

8 Cut platinum wire so that it is 0.5 mm shorter than the outside of the posts. Insert the rivet through the posts and lentil, then solder each end of the rivet with 18k yellow gold hard solder, concealing the rivet. Be careful not to flow solder through the shank and onto the lentil.

9 Cut the posts to the desired height. (See Diagram F on page 69.) Polish the ring. Set the 2.2 mm diamonds in the ends of the posts, using the tube setting techniques described on pages 59–61. *Note: Smaller diamonds may be flush-set into the lentil.*

MARIANNE HUNTER

Photo by Brian Groggin

"My artwork is very personal," says enamel and metal artist Marianne Hunter. "Each piece tells a story that evolves while I am working. When my jewelry comes out of the fire for the last time, the story is complete." Driven by a passionate yearning for self-expression, Marianne creates each item as a unique entity complete with a poem/title, date of completion, sequential number, and signature, all engraved on the back.

Marianne came to jewelry as a painter and crafts explorer in the 1960's. When a friend gave her the equipment for enamel work, but no instructions, she decided to teach herself, and developed a method for creating black-and-white images, using the grisaille technique. Later, adding color and metallic foils to her work, "It gave me a euphoric sense of limitlessness," she recalls.

Many years later, Marianne looks at what she does with a more global sophistication. "I see enamels, metals, and gems as separate instruments working in concert," Marianne says. "The central enamel image is the melody, which I embellish with finely detailed metalwork. Other materials, ranging from fossils to diamonds and colored gems, are used as a refrain or counterpoint to the enamels' theme." Her goal is to orchestrate the work, to create a compelling and complete composition, unified and supported by complex layers of detail.

Marianne's jewelry is painstakingly created in an arduous series of steps. Each piece begins with a metal structure over which 3–5 firings of black enamel are laid. The images are then built up in very thin layers of enamel applied dry by sifting or spreading with a fine knife. Foils of pure gold (24k) and pure silver are cut into precise shapes according to her drawings. These are fired into place over previously-fired layers and are further covered with successive layers of transparent enamels. Bezels for the gems as well as most other decorative elements are made of pure gold, while supporting structures and clasps are made of 18k and 14k gold and/or sterling silver to give strength and color variation. A finished piece can require as many as 80 firings, after which exposed metal surfaces are textured to reflect light, while adding to the overall richness of the work. It is understandable that each piece takes Marianne up to three weeks to complete. The sustaining motive for Marianne's work is the never-ending discovery of the beauty and mystery of life.

Marianne Hunter

Photo by Hap Sakwa

Kabuki Kachina Calls for the Winds of Eventide.

AVALON

A channel crossing to Catalina Island as well as a selection of unique opals provided the inspiration for this necklace. The artist has inscribed the following poem on the back:
Avalon, beguiling Isle of enchanted journeys and bewitching waters! Shall we keep watch for fish that fly or be lulled to sleep by singing dolphins?
Summer 1997

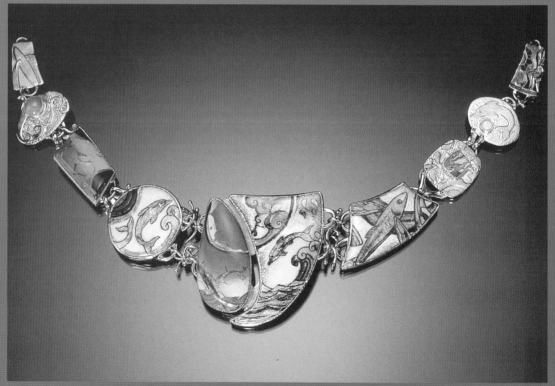

Photo by Hap Sakwa

AVALON

Materials		Measurements
	Enamels in various colors	80 grit
	Australian boulder opals	
	Citron chrysoprase	
	Turquoise	
24k	Gold sheet	0.3 mm (28 gauge)
18k	Green gold sheet	0.5 mm (24 gauge)
14k	Yellow gold round wire	1 mm (18 gauge); 0.8 mm (20 gauge)
	Sterling silver sheet	0.6 mm (22 gauge)
	Copper sheet	1 mm (18 gauge)
24k	Gold foil	
	Sterling silver foil	
	Enamel oil	
18k	Yellow gold chain	

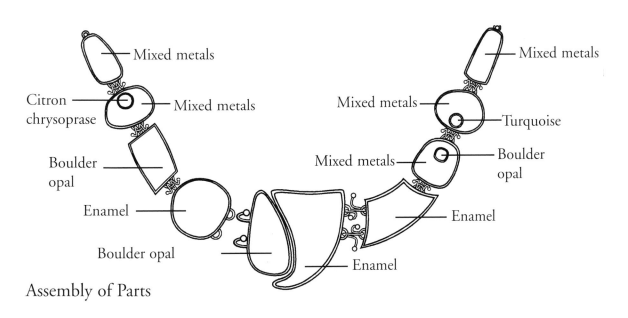

Assembly of Parts

AVALON

Dawn Collar   Photo by Hap Sakwa

1 Select and arrange a suite of boulder opals. Choose the major stone for its natural image. Shapes are designed to complement and contrast the major stones in order to create a rhythm that is syncopated and pleasing. Make sketches with the main enamel piece integrated with the central opal.

2 Transfer the sketches for the enamel sections to a sheet of 1 mm copper sheet. Use a saw to pierce these bases. File and sand bases.

3 Use a sable brush to coat the top surfaces of the bases with a thin layer of specialized enameling oil. Sift finely powdered 80 grit black enamel in a thin but complete layer onto the surface of each section. Fire the bases to vitrify the enamels, heating the enamel converts it to glass.

4 Check the surfaces. Use a file to reveal bubbles and open them up. Recoat with oil and add more black enamel. Refire until the surface is perfect. In the same manner, build up several layers of opaque ivory-colored enamel over the black, until a dense and even layer is achieved.

5 Begin shading with opaque and transparent 80 grit enamels onto areas which will not be covered by foil. Apply the colors in thin layers, always over a light coating of oil. Apply enamels either by sifting through a screen or by transporting tiny amounts of enamel to the desired locations with a small spatula or knife. Fire each successive layer and cool.

6 At this point, the bases should be counter enameled (enameled on the back) to prevent cracking on the front. Turn the work over, add some oil and a thin layer of any kind of enamel to the back. Handling the piece by the edges, turn it right side up and place into a trivet. From this point onward, all firing takes place in a trivet that holds the work by the edges. Fire the work again.

7 Cut pieces of sterling silver and 24k gold foil (not leaf) and place them in position with a small amount of enamel oil. Fire briefly to adhere the foil. Cool and apply more oil, followed by clear enamel. Fire and cool again. Colored enamels are layered over the foil in several firings to intensify the effect. Repeat until all of the enamel components are complete.

8 Begin to make bezels for the enamels and gems by cutting strips of 0.3 mm 24k gold sheet, about one millimeter wider than the height of each element. Form each individual bezel around the shape with your fingers. Adjust the ends and either solder or fuse the bezels closed. Place them onto a backing of 0.6 mm sterling silver sheet and use silver medium solder to join them.

9 Cut out the required sections of 0.6 mm sterling silver sheet for the components without enamel. Add shapes in 0.3 mm 24k gold, and 0.5 mm 18k green gold sheet, and solder to silver bases. Polish, engrave, and texture as per the design.

10 Use sections of 1 mm gold round wire for the connections between the elements. Form the connectors into horseshoe-shaped loops, which are gently forged and soldered to the backs of the bezels with silver easy solder.

11 Use annealed sections of gold round wire in various thicknesses to weave the pieces together, each in a different way. Attach two sections of gold chain, one to each end of the necklace, with a catch in between.

12 Give the metal a fine finish and add an inscription on the back with a vibro-engraver.

13 Set the stones and enamels carefully within the bezels and burnish to secure. Add textures to the bezels with a scribe. Polish with rouge.

Photo by G. Post

Kabuki Kachina Wears a Coat of Many Colors

Photo by G. Post

Harmony

Photo by Hap Sakwa

Lady of Lotus

TIM McCREIGHT

Few professional crafts people started out to be what they are today. Kids want to be firemen or doctors or astronauts—teacher of jewelry is not on most kid's lists. And it wasn't on Tim McCreight's, though that's what he's done for the last twenty years. Tim went to a liberal arts school, The College of Wooster, in the early 70s. There he took classes in history, philosophy, English, science, and art. When it came time to choose a major it was a hard call. Everything held equal interest for him.

In the end it was a combination of factors that brought Tim to jewelry design. "I really enjoyed everything about it; the process of making, the blend of function and design, the connection with a wearer. And, of course, the fact that it could be easily stored, shipped, and sold didn't hurt," he says.

Tim graduated with a degree in sculpture, having taught himself jewelry making along the way. Tim then went to Bowling Green State University where he studied under Hal Hasselschwert and Chuck Evans. It was here that his love of teaching was confirmed. Tim taught a general art education course for freshmen. "I'd always known I enjoyed being in front of a group," he recalls, "but it was here that I realized this could be part of my life. I still wasn't thinking a lot about the future, but I came to realize that there were more ways to make a living in crafts than just selling your work."

By the time he earned his MFA in 1975, Tim was convinced he wanted to teach. He eagerly sent out his résumé and watched with anxiety as nothing happened. He and his wife Jay had a newborn daughter, an eagerness to relocate, and exactly zero prospects. They packed their bags, dogs, studio, and child and moved to Vermont. Eventually the Worcester Craft Center in Massachusetts offered Tim a full-time position. That was in the fall of 1976 and he's been teaching ever since. He currently heads the Metals Department at Maine College of Art in Portland.

Tim is widely known for his books on jewelry making, knife making, casting, rendering, and design. His most successful book, *The Complete Metalsmith*, took Tim three years to research, personally test every bit of information and then hand-letter the original. "Publishing propels my own education and it contributes to my teaching."

Pendant

Tim also runs a publishing company and is always involved in several projects. He is a consultant for Mitsubishi Materials of Japan, the inventor of a product called Precious Metal Clay.

Despite a schedule that would be difficult for three people to fill, Tim still makes one-of-a-kind work at his bench. Tim is exploring new ways to bring the pleasure of jewelry to an even wider audience.

76

STERLING BEAD

As much an exercise in process as instruction in making a bead, the project takes an unusual approach to fabrication. Tim uses punches to poke holes, and tabbing systems to create joints, both of which are uncommon procedures for jewelry. The result is a precisely-created, primitive-looking pendant that escapes common concepts about fine jewelry. Like much of his jewelry, this piece proudly shows the marks left by the process of its construction.

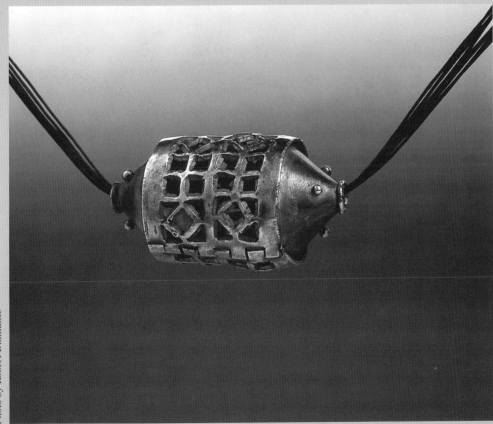

Photo by Robert Diamante

STERLING BEAD

Materials		*Measurements*
	Sterling silver sheet	0.8 mm (20 gauge) x 9.2 mm wide x 50 mm long
	Sterling silver wire	1.5 mm (15 gauge) x 14 mm long - 2 pieces
14k	Yellow gold wire scrap	

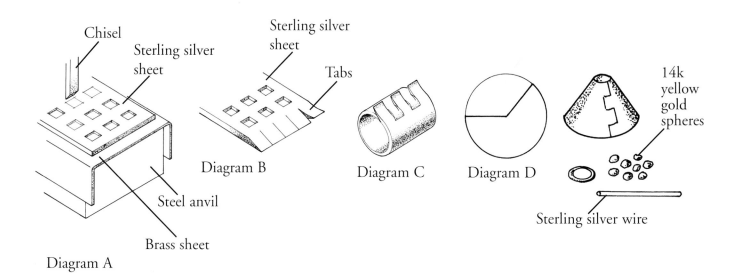

Diagram A

Diagram B

Diagram C

Diagram D

14k yellow gold spheres

Sterling silver wire

STERLING BEAD

1 Either begin with a piece of sterling silver sheet, the correct thickness, or forge down a thicker sheet to 0.8 mm.

2 Anneal a 9 mm x 50 mm piece of 0.8 mm sterling silver sheet. Place it onto a scrap of brass sheet that is covering an anvil. Use a razor-sharp chisel to pierce the sheet, in this case creating a geometric grille. (See Diagram A above.)

3 Thin the two opposing sides by forging, to prepare them for joining.

Photo by Robert Diamante

Precious Metal Clay Pin

Photo by Robert Diamante

Beach Pebble Pendant

4   Cut tabs at the edges and offset them so that when the form is rolled into a cylinder the edges meet like fingers of two clasped hands. (See Diagram B on page 78.)

5   Form the panel around a cylindrical mandrel and tap the fingers down to secure the shape. (See Diagram C on page 78.) Use silver hard solder to join the seam.

6   Make two cones in a similar manner, each from a pie-shaped section of sterling silver sheet. Solder them closed and onto the ends of the perforated tube. (See Diagram D on page 78.)

7   Cut a strip of sterling silver sheet and hammer it into a concave tool called a swage block (also called a design block) to create a length of wire.

8   Bend the sterling silver wire into circles and solder them to the cones.

9   Fuse eight small spheres from the gold scrap wire and solder them to the cones.

10   Pickle, rinse, dry, and apply a liver-of-sulfur patina to "oxidize" the surface. Polish by hand.

Photo by Robert Diamante

Sterling Fibula

Photo by Robert Diamante

Yellow Gold Fibula

DON FRIEDLICH

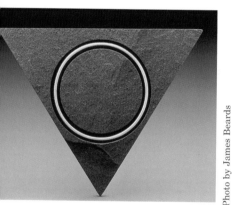

Translucence Series Brooch

Photo by David Trawicks

Photo by James Beards

Don Friedlich was the type of child who wanted to know what made things tick. His specialty was household appliances, many of which he took apart and few of which ever ran again. Don said he was trying to "repair" them. To everyone's delight, a few gadgets actually survived the ordeal with improved performance. "Thomas Edison was my idol," Don recalls. "His laboratory in Menlo Park was near where we lived, in New Jersey." One of Don's prized possessions is an autographed portrait of Thomas Edison. Don knew where he was headed, or at least he thought so at the time, "I wanted to be an inventor when I grew up."

By his late teens, Don was disillusioned with science—out of college, without focus, and ski-bumming in Vermont. On the slopes Don met a local jeweler and they became friends. That summer, while visiting Martha's Vineyard, Don found a smooth water-polished stone on the beach. "I brought it back and asked my friend to make it into a piece of jewelry for me. She refused, but offered to show me how." The rest, as they say, is precious history.

"In making jewelry," Don explains, "my mechanical skills merged with a creative impulse I never knew I had." Knowing the value of a proper training, Don set out to get an education that would expand and refine his ability to make jewelry. He took art and jewelry classes at the University of Vermont, workshops at Haystack Mountain School of Crafts, and wound up with a Bachelor of Fine Arts degree in Jewelry and Metalsmithing from Rhode Island School of Design (RISD). Three years later, he was honored as the school's outstanding recent graduate.

Don's work has been on the cutting edge on several fronts. "Both slate and glass pieces are studies in contrast. They are, at once, rough and smooth, geometric and organic, precious and nonprecious, traditional and experimental." The result is dramatic and captivating. As the wearer moves, the color of each **FRIEDLICH** glass piece appears to change, exploiting the dynamic optical qualities of glass. Don's jewelry has a monumental reference, but the scale he uses is intimate and appropriate for the human body.

Photo by David Trawick

GLASS BROOCH

Don's one-of-a-kind brooches are fine jewelry. They are craft, and they are art. The distinction between those otherwise fairly identifiable fields blurs when viewing his work. Don carves ordinary clear glass, using techniques usually reserved for fine gems. The glass is set over niobium, a metal that is vibrantly colored through the application of electricity. He then employs goldsmithing techniques to detail and finish the work.

GLASS BROOCH

Materials		Measurements
	Pyrex glass pane	4.7 mm
	Sterling silver sheet	0.6 mm (22 gauge)
22k	Yellow gold bezel strip	0.5 mm (24 gauge), 4 mm wide
	Niobium sheet	0.5 mm
	Sterling silver pin joint and catch with nickel rivet and pin stem	

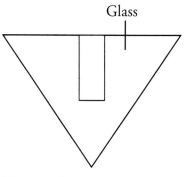

Glass

Diagram A

Diagram B

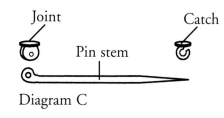

Joint

Catch

Pin stem

Diagram C

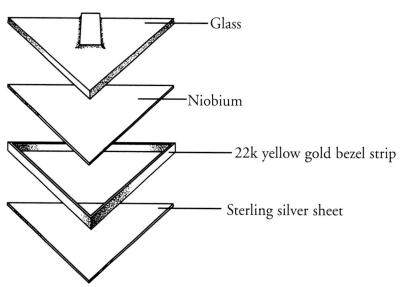

Glass

Niobium

22k yellow gold bezel strip

Sterling silver sheet

Assembly of Parts

Interference Series Brooch

Photo by James Beards

GLASS BROOCH

1 With a permanent marker, draw an isosceles triangle onto the glass approximately 65 mm on two sides and 70 mm on the third side. (See Diagram A on page 82.)

2 Scribe the triangle with a glass cutter. Wearing leather gloves to protect your hands, break the glass at the scribe marks.

3 Smooth the edges of the triangle with a wet diamond or silicon carbide lapidary drum sander (approximately 220 grit). Slightly, round all the edges where the cut sides meet the flat surface of the glass. Do not round the points of the triangle.

4 Set a combination square against the triangle's long edge and, using a pencil, mark the rectangular design on the surface of a heavy sandblasting mask-out, available through gravestone carvers' or glass artists' supply houses.

5 Cut the mask-out with an sharp blade, peeling away the excess so the surface design remains covered while the rest of the glass is exposed. Cover the back with another piece of mask-out.

6 Wearing safety goggles and a respirator, use a powerful sandblaster, charged with 120–220 aluminum oxide abrasive, to carve away the exposed glass to half its original thickness. Remove the mask-out from the front surface only.

7 Using a fine-grit, flat, diamond file, bevel the edges of the raised portion of the glass, followed by 220, 400, and 600 grit sandpaper. With the wet belt, bevel the edges of the triangle to about a 70° angle. (See Diagram B on page 82.)

8 Wrap the gold bezel strip around the glass, bending each corner with flat pliers. The bezel should

fit closely, with the seam in the middle of the top edge. Solder or fuse the seam of the bezel.

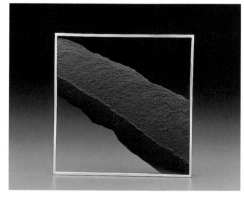

Interference Series Brooch

9   File both sides of the soldered seam, then sand smooth with 600 grit abrasive paper. Anneal the bezel.

10 Cut the sterling silver sheet so that it is about 5 mm larger than the glass on all sides.

11 Solder the triangular gold bezel strip to the silver sheet with silver hard or medium solder. Air cool, then pickle clean.

12 Sweat silver easy solder onto the two parts of the pin findings, then sweat in place onto the silver back. Air cool, then pickle clean. (See Diagram C on page 82.)

13 Trim the overhanging silver sheet with a jeweler's saw. File smooth, then sand with up to 600 grit abrasive paper.

14 Finish the brooch by roller printing a piece of niobium sheet against a piece of ribbon or fabric. Trim the sheet the same size as the glass.

15 Anodize the niobium to a golden yellow color. Fit the niobium and glass into the setting. *Note: The gold bezel strip will be too high at this stage in the process.*

16 Mark the inside of the bezel strip by running a scribe gently along the glass surface. Remove the glass and niobium. Use a shear to trim the bezel strip a little below your scribe line.

17 Polish the setting fully, cleaning all the surfaces.

Organic Series Bead Necklace

18 Place the niobium and glass in the setting and burnish the bezel down to secure the glass in place.

19 Crimp the pin stem in place by squeezing the rivet with parallel pliers.

84

JACLYN DAVIDSON

Goddess Necklace

Photo by Allen Bryan

It was almost as if crafts were re-invented in the 1960's. Prior to that, no one in their right mind thought about abandoning academia and job security for the unsteady life of a crafts artist. Perhaps it was that turbulent decade and the reaction it caused, that freed a generation to look outside the envelope. If so, Jaclyn Davidson was one of the chosen, and American culture the ultimate beneficiary.

In a world which moves farther and farther away from the personal and toward social security numbers, actuarial tables, screen names, and PIN codes, no one can deny that we seem to be losing touch with our intuitive, nonrational qualities. For Jaclyn Davidson, jewelry provides a connection between people, ideas, and cultures. "I am interested in objects that are intimate and personal, and jewelry has these qualities," says Jackie, as she carves a small animal in wax. "Alienation is rampant, but jewelry provides a vehicle for people to return to an instinctual, almost primitive relationship with each other and with Earth," says the artist.

Jaclyn's role as facilitator began in college. As an art major, she was required to take an elective crafts class. In order to decide which one to take, she wandered from studio to studio checking them all out. Winding down the stairs to the basement of the art building, she stepped into the jewelry workshop for the first time. "That was it!" she recalls. "I was fascinated by the paraphernalia, the minutia, the potential. I wanted to know what every tool did." And so, like many others, Jaclyn found herself immersed in jewelry.

"It is important to me that my pieces have a life of their own apart from their role as wearable objects and personal adornment," explains the artist. "My designs originate from things that I have read or heard people say, as much as from what I have seen. The visual contents often illustrate a story rooted in mythology or folklore. Once I begin to work on an idea, the design may lose touch with its origin and follow its own dynamic route, often resulting in unusual or absurd juxtapositions."

"My jewelry is also an anchor," Jackie explains. "It must be more than ornament. It needs to touch something on a mythical, familial, spiritual level."

These days Jaclyn can be found in her isolated studio, nestled in the quiet woods of Vermont, where she lives with her husband and two children. Her shelves are lined with books, reflecting the wide range of her interests and the stimuli for her work—Kafka and Lalique, Hesse and Fabergé, Camus and Eskimo art.

Photo by J. David Long

POND BRACELET

Photo by Allen Bryan

This photograph shows two views of the elaborate Pond Bracelet. This complex piece is composed of cast and fabricated elements embellished with engraving and enameling. The bracelet consists of two cast 18k gold inserts set into two fabricated sterling silver housings plus a clasp and hinge. One insert is built up and carved in high relief, and the other is carved in low relief and enameled, using the base taille technique (filling in recessed textured areas with translucent enamel).

POND BRACELET

Materials		Measurements
18k	Yellow gold casting shot	
	Hard green carving wax	1 mm thick (18 gauge)
	Soft brown "sticky wax"	lump form
	Sterling silver sheet	1 mm (18 gauge)
	Sterling silver rod	4 mm (6 gauge)
	Sterling silver tubing	5 mm outside diameter x 0.5 mm wall
	Sterling silver discs	0.8 mm (20 gauge): 5 mm diameter - 1 piece; 3 mm diameter - 1 piece; 1.6 mm (14 gauge): 5 mm diameter - 1 piece
14k	White gold wire	1.6 mm (14 gauge) square; 1.3 mm (16 gauge) round; 1 mm (18 gauge) round
	Blue enamel powder	

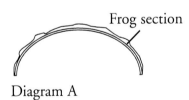

Diagram A

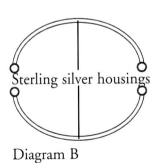

Diagram B

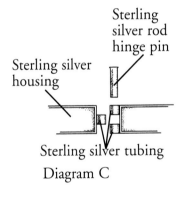

Diagram C

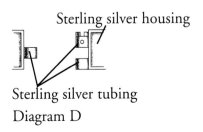

Diagram D

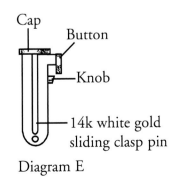

Diagram E

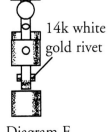

Diagram F

POND BRACELET

1 The intricate design for this complex bracelet includes images of sea animals: carp swimming, turtles and frogs climbing over each other. Begin with a detailed sketch of both halves of the bracelet. Transfer the designs onto a piece of paper in actual size showing all details.

2 Cut a piece of hard green carving wax (flat) for the low relief of the swimming carp, which will be enameled. This portion is prepared flat and then curved after casting. Taper the pieces so that the ends are 13 mm wide and the middle of the strip is 15 mm wide. Paint the wax with thick white watercolor paint. Place the drawing of this section over a piece of carbon paper. Use a ballpoint pen to transfer the pattern to the wax.

3 Cut the outline of the carp design into the hard wax with a blade, leaving a 1 mm border along the sides of the wax strip. Use gravers to cut the background away to a low relief, leaving a flat base about 0.5 mm thick. Use gravers to cut a swirling background pattern onto the base. When the enamel is added, this will show through and look like blue water.

Photo by Allen Bryan

Fish Brooch

4 The soft wax is worked in a different manner entirely. Take a portion of the wax and form it into a strip, about 1 mm thick x 15 mm wide x 100 mm long. Taper the ends as above. Wrap the strip around a leather-covered (because the wax will not stick) bracelet form.

5 Taking small pieces of the soft wax, shape and carve them into turtles and frogs. Refine them by a combination of carving and building, using a variety of tools, such as gravers, knives, and scrapers.

6 Add the animals to the strip, climbing over and under each other in high relief. Heat the base with a hot needle to join the animals. (See Diagram A on page 87.)

7 Thin both wax models from behind to 0.9 mm. The hard wax half is thinned easily, using a coarse ball bur held in a flexible-shaft machine. Leave a 1 mm border along the edge. Hold the wax up to a bright light and carve from the back. When part of the wax is carved down to the thickness desired (as measured by a spring gauge) use the color and intensity of this translucence as a guide for thinning the rest of the piece.

8 The soft wax is trickier to thin because a bur will clog and cannot be used. Instead, use a knife-like scraper (the kind used by dentists works well) to scrape off excess material.

Photo by Allen Bryan

9 When both halves are refined, sprue, invest, and cast them in 18k yellow gold. After casting, clip the sprues and form the carp unit over a bracelet mandrel to match the frog unit.

10 File a slight bevel on the sides of both units for setting into housings.

11 Fabricate the two housings from 1 mm sterling silver sheet to cradle the inserts. (See Diagram B on page 87.) These should match the inserts. When complete, sand, buff, and scrub, using a brass brush, with a mixture of liquid soap and hot water with a few drops of ammonia.

12 Purchase or make tubes for the hinge and clasp from 5 mm sterling silver tubing. For a three-knuckle hinge, each section should be 5 mm long. Solder the tube sections in place on the hinge side with two outer hinge knuckles on one housing half and the matching center knuckle in place on the mating end. (See Diagram C on page 87.)

Brooch 13

13 For the clasp, each section should be 4.2 mm long. Recess the tubing 2.4 mm from the end. Solder a 1.6 mm x 5 mm diameter sterling silver disc as a cap onto the end of the recessed tubing. File and sand. Cut or file a groove in the cap perpendicular to the bracelet to accommodate the clasp pin. Drill a 1.3 mm hole below the groove. (See Diagram D on page 87.)

14 Use 1.6 mm 14k white gold square wire for the sliding clasp pin. (See Diagram E on page 87.) This hard, springy alloy is chosen for function and durability. Make a crisp 90° "L" bend near one end of the wire. Make a "U" bend about 12 mm from the first bend, so that the piece slides into the top clasp tubing with the bottom of the "U" almost reaching the end of the bottom tubing.

15 Use 14k white gold hard solder to fill in part of the "U", providing space for a hole. Insert the pin into the clasp tubing. Mark the hole location on the sliding pin. Remove the pin and solder a 1.3 mm piece of 14k white gold round wire at the marked location. (See Diagram E on page 87.) Trim this wire knob at an angle so that it slips into the hole in the tubing. Adjust the fit so that the pin stops as the knob snaps into the hole.

16 Insert and trim the long straight end of the sliding pin flush with the top clasp section. Solder a 0.8 mm x 5 mm sterling silver disc as a cap onto the end of the sliding pin. Trim

Photo by Allen Bryan

Brooch 12

Pendant Necklace

Photo by Allen Bryan

the "L," leaving enough to allow for complete insertion to the point where the knob is freed from the hole. Solder a 0.8 mm x 3 mm sterling silver disc onto the end of the "L", as a button.

17 Drill a 1 mm hole in the bottom of the "U". Insert the sliding pin into the tubing and place a 2.6 mm long section of 1 mm 14k white gold round wire into the hole in the "U". Upset the ends to form a rivet, which prevents the sliding pin from being withdrawn completely. (See Diagram F on page 87.)

18 Set the hinge pin by inserting the 4 mm sterling silver rod into the tube sections, locking the housings in place. Saw or file the ends of the hinge pin to about 0.5 mm longer than the hinge on each end. Use a cross-peen hammer to upset the ends of the pin.

19 Prepare the low-relief carp unit for enameling. Heat the piece with a torch and pickle it to leave the surface chemically clean for enameling.

20 Brush the carp unit with a clean wet brass brush to achieve a bright satin finish. Clean the enamel powder with distilled water and apply to the recessed areas. Allow to dry, then place it in a kiln and fire the enamel until the surface is glossy. Remove, cool very slowly, pickle to remove oxidation and rinse in baking soda/water solution (1 part to 2 parts H_2O). Stone the surface under running water to level off uneven portions. Repack areas where more enamel is needed and repeat this sequence about four times, until the enamel forms a clean, even surface. After the enameling is complete, refinish the pieces with a very light polish.

21 Add the fine detail on the carp side by engraving.

22 Slip the units into the housings with either a burnisher, pusher, or punch. Close the edges of the silver housings inward to lock the inserts in place.

23 Brass-brush the metal while it is wet for the final satin finish.

THOMAS HERMAN

Thomas Herman grew up on a family farm in Minnesota. When he was five years old, he was involved in a machinery accident and lost three fingers on his right hand. Tom learned to adapt quickly, realizing that if he ignored his disability, everyone else would, too. Obviously, this approach worked and Tom wound up choosing a career that requires the highest level of manual dexterity.

Tom's favorite subject was art. By chance, his school offered a segment on jewelry making and it was here that Tom was shown how to saw, solder, sand, and file silver. Momentum alone (not his grades) carried Tom to the University of Iowa. Tom was far from academically inclined. When asked what he learned in college, Tom replies with typical honesty, "I learned how to party!"

Photo by Ralph Gabriner

Tanzanite Earrings

Unfortunately, grades were not given in that subject and at age nineteen, Tom found himself out of school and on his own. The next fall, Tom enrolled in a college program called Campus on Wheels, in which a group of students and teachers traveled across North America in buses. Tom learned a lot about the world and about himself on the trip. He met artisans and craftsmen, and for the first time in his life, he thought about working with his hands.

He got the idea to open a small jewelry store. "I must have been crazy," Tom says now with a few decades of sanity behind him. "I didn't have the skills to be a jeweler and I knew nothing about business, but I had a lot of desire and very supportive parents. The next thing I knew, I was the owner of "Emerald City."

After a four-year education as a maker/merchant, Tom closed the shop and drove to San Francisco where he got a job with Van Craeynest and Company, one of the city's oldest and finest manufacturers. For the next four years, Tom worked in this museum-like shrine to fine craftsmanship. Looking back Tom says, "I should have paid them for what I learned."

Photo by Susan Herman

In his free time, Tom pursued his own work which he first exhibited at a craft show during a summer vacation. Selling nearly every piece he brought inspired his transition to self-employment, and Seven Fingers Jewelry was born.

Tom now creates one-of-a-kind jewelry, which, he sells directly to the public at top national craft fairs.

PALM FROND BROOCH

Photo by Ralph Gabriner

This piece was inspired by the work of René Lalique, considered by many to be the supreme master of Art Nouveau jewelry. This brooch combines the techniques of wax carving and casting, fabrication, chasing, and gem carving. Looking to the future, Tom sees himself putting more time and materials into fewer pieces. "I want to create finer and more elaborate jewelry, reminiscent of the great jewelers of the past," states Herman.

PALM FROND BROOCH

Materials		*Measurements*
18k	Yellow gold casting shot	
18k	Yellow gold sheet	1.5 mm (15 gauge); 1 mm (18 gauge); 0.8 mm (20 gauge); 0.4 mm (26 gauge)
18k	Yellow gold wire	0.8 mm
	Stainless steel wire	0.8 mm
18k	Yellow gold pin catch	
	Sagenite	37 mm x 27 mm

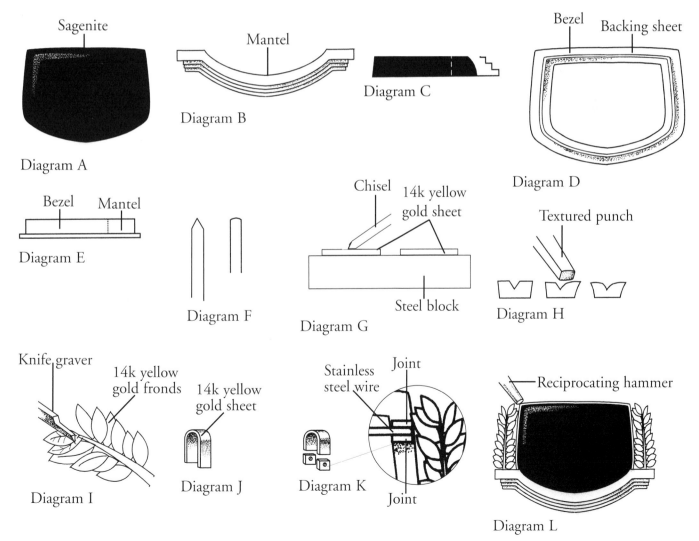

Sagenite

Diagram A

Mantel

Diagram B

Diagram C

Bezel   Backing sheet

Diagram D

Bezel   Mantel

Diagram E

Diagram F

Chisel   14k yellow gold sheet

Steel block

Diagram G

Textured punch

Diagram H

Knife graver   14k yellow gold fronds   14k yellow gold sheet

Diagram I

Diagram J

Stainless steel wire   Joint

Diagram K

Joint

Reciprocating hammer

Diagram L

PALM FROND BROOCH

1 Traditional lapidary techniques are used to cut a piece of sagenite: slicing, cutting, grinding, sanding, and polishing. (See Diagram A on page 93.) Sagenite is a variety of quartz with small brown needle-like inclusions. Carve a wax mantel to fit the stone, hollowing the back to an even thickness. (See Diagram B on page 93.)

2 Cast the mantel in 18k yellow gold. File the casting to fit the stone. The stone should slip into the mantel where it will be held with a bezel. (See Diagram C on page 93.)

Laurel and Ginko Motifs

Photo by Ralph Gabriner

3 Make a bezel for the stone, using a strip 0.4 mm gold sheet, 5 mm wide. Solder it to a slightly larger sheet of gold 0.8 mm thick. Saw out the interior of the sheet, leaving a seat about 2 mm wide. Trim the outside of the bezel. The open back lets light show through the translucent stone. (See Diagram D on page 93.)

4 With the stone in the mantel, measure and mark how much of the bezel to cut away so that it fits against the mantel. Trim and solder the bezel to the mantel. (See Diagram E on page 93.)

5 Use a soft-lead pencil to lay out palm frond designs on two pieces 1.5 mm gold sheet 20 mm x 10 mm. Use a fast glue to adhere these to a smooth block of steel. This is the simplest holding devise to support the gold while chasing.

6 Use a small line chisel and chasing hammer to define the palm fronds. This sharp punch has a slightly curved top with even bevels on both sides. (See Diagram F on page 93.) Go back over the pattern and cut deeply, raising the edges of the leaves to create the illusion of overlapping. (See Diagram G on page 93.) Use a #6 onglette graver to remove some gold from the center of each leaf.

7 Prepare a textured planishing punch by pounding it into sandpaper, a sharpening stone, or a diamond file to pick up texture. This punch has a rectangular face and is very slightly domed so it will "walk" or slide along, embellishing a surface without digging into the metal. Use this punch to smooth out the surface and give the final texture to the leaves. (See Diagram H on page 93.)

8 Heat the gold with a torch to break the glue bond. Drill holes, then use a saw to pierce around the palm fronds and through where the leaves attach to the stem. Reglue and rechase the fonds, refining the pattern and adding more detail. Use a #1 knife graver to add lines to the leaves. (See Diagram I on page 93.)

9 Solder the palm fronds to the bezel/mantel.

10 Add findings to the back. For the joint, use 1 mm gold sheet, 4 mm x 10 mm bent into a "U"-shape. (See Diagram J on page 93.) Drill two 0.8 mm holes near the bases. After soldering it in place, cut off the top, leaving two perfectly parallel walls that serve as a joint for the pin. (See Diagram K on page 93.) Solder a pin catch on the other side. Add a pin stem of 0.8 mm polished stainless steel wire with a loop bent on one end. Shape and polish the point, then rivet the pin stem into the joint with a piece of 0.8 mm gold wire.

11 Set the stone by pushing the bezel in and over with a reciprocating hammer hand piece for the flex-shaft. Start in the corners, then close in the sides. Tighten and smooth the edges with a burnisher. (See Diagram L on page 93.)

12 Shape and finish the bezel with a pumice wheel. (Pumice will not scratch the stone.) Finally, polish the bezel and the rest of the piece as necessary.

Lalique-inspired Brooch

Photo by Ralph Gabriner

Brooch with acanthus leaf scrolls

Photo by Ralph Gabriner

CHARLES LEWTON-BRAIN

BRAIN BRAIN Master goldsmith Charles Lewton-Brain has a worldly view of things. He was born in London, but spent his early years in Tanzania (East Africa), where his parents were an anthropologist and a nurse in the British colonial service. Charles finished high school in New York, then moved to Germany's Black Forest so he could study with the region's renowned goldsmiths and silversmiths. Since 1986, Charles and his wife, Dee Fontans, have lived in Canada, where they both teach jewelry and metalsmithing.

Photo by Bob McCrae

A life-long fascination with metal and his childlike drive to explore the world around him, drove Charles to pursue a formal metals education. He trained in Pforzheim, Germany, with Klaus Ullrich—a celebrated designer, master goldsmith, and master silversmith. This was followed by a stint at State University of New York in New Paltz. There, Charles conducted research on fold-forming, while earning a Master of Fine Arts degree under Kurt Matzdorf and Bob Ebendorf.

Internationally known and respected within his field, Charles has written and published several unique jewelry books. He teaches in the Jewelry/Metals program at Canada's Alberta College of Art and Design, and he travels around the world teaching metals and jewelry skills to some of today's most creative artisans.

Perhaps Charles' most significant contribution has been to invent a way of working metal that never existed before. He named these techniques fold-forming. As amazing as it may seem, no one has ever approached metal this way during the 10,000-year history of the craft. The concept is to crease and fold a piece of metal, as one would paper, and then selectively forge, form, roll, and unfold it to produce light, elegant volumetric shapes. The dynamic and fascinating forms created through this system are unachievable by any other technique.

"Through my studies and travels, I have come to appreciate the magic that is possible if you understand the nature of materials," says Charles. "My work is concerned with process, beauty, and function, while always seeking to unlock metal's innate nature. If you know what metal 'wants' to do, you can utilize that tendency to create work of inherently natural

Photo by Charles Lewton-Brain

beauty." Much like the sculptor, who releases a form hiding in rock, Charles views his role as the liberator of metal—watching, feeling, and listening closely to his materials for insight and guidance.

Charles summarizes his love affair with metal saying, "The best part about being a goldsmith is that every time I walk into the workshop there is something new to discover."

Shell Earrings

SNAKE BROOCH

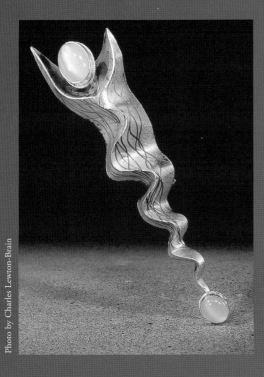

Photo by Charles Lewton-Brain

This unusual piece demonstrates one of the basic fold-forming techniques developed by Charles. The patterned metal is created from a precious metal laminate of 18k yellow gold and sterling silver, a material available from some suppliers. The metal is engraved, rolled, embossed, cut, scored, creased, folded, soldered, punched, drilled, sawed, filed, brushed, blackened, set with gems, and polished, demonstrating a virtual encyclopedia of metalsmithing technique.

SNAKE BROOCH

Materials		*Measurements*
24k	Gold sheet	0.3 mm (28 gauge) x 3 mm
	Sterling silver sheet	1.2 mm (16 gauge)
18k	Yellow gold laminated on sterling sheet	0.8 mm (20 gauge)
	(This material can correctly be called "gold filled," "rolled gold," or 18k gold "doublée".)	
	Sterling silver pin findings	
	Moonstones	2 pieces

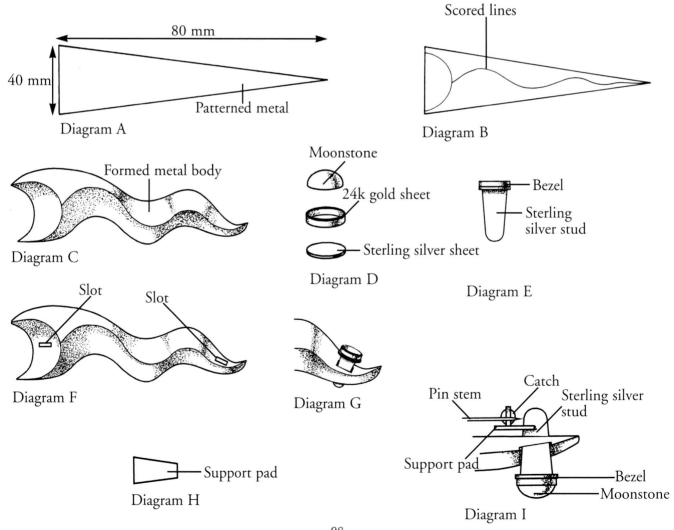

80 mm

40 mm

Patterned metal

Diagram A

Scored lines

Diagram B

Formed metal body

Diagram C

Moonstone

24k gold sheet

Sterling silver sheet

Diagram D

Bezel

Sterling silver stud

Diagram E

Slot   Slot

Diagram F

Diagram G

Pin stem   Catch   Sterling silver stud

Support pad

Bezel
Moonstone

Diagram I

Support pad

Diagram H

SNAKE BROOCH

1   Begin with a piece of 0.8 mm gold/silver laminated sheet. In preparation for creating a colored surface pattern, engrave or abrade through the gold layer to expose the silver beneath.

2   Use a rolling mill to reduce the thickness to 0.5 mm and flatten the metal.

3   Make a paper "die" by cutting shapes into a manila folder cover with a sharp blade. Place the die against the gold side of the metal, with a sheet of folded paper towel against the silver side. Put the stack in a rolling mill. Find a tight setting (practice first) and then roll the stack through. The metal is squeezed into the cavities in the die, leaving an embossed 3-D relief.

4   From this material, cut a triangle for the body of the brooch and anneal it. (See Diagram A on page 98.)

Gem Scape

5   Draw bend lines on the back (the silver side of the laminate) with a pencil. Place a silicon carbide separating disc in a flex-shaft and, WEARING GOGGLES, cut into the metal slowly and carefully along the lines. Practice on scrap first. (See Diagram B on page 98.)

6   The scored lines are weak. With gentle finger pressure, crimp the sides inward to transform the metal from two to three dimensions. Flux and use silver hard solder on the interior of the scored seams for strength. (See Diagram C on page 98.)

7   Bend strips of gold sheet around the stones, cut to fit and fuse or solder with 20k yellow gold. Solder these with silver hard solder onto the 1.2 mm sterling silver sheet. Cut out the bezel shape from the sheet, leaving a small lip as ornament. Use a saw or file to cut ornamental notches into the silver at the base. (See Diagram D on page 98.)

8   From the sterling silver sheet, cut two 4 mm x 10 mm studs and solder to the bezels. (See Diagram E on page 98.)

9   Layout two slots in the body for the studs. Use a center punch, then drill, saw, and file as necessary to adjust the slots to fit the studs. (See Diagram F on page 98.)

10   Insert the studs and solder them in place. These protrude through the metal to the back to provide locations for the findings. (See Diagram G on page 98.)

Photo by Charles Lewton-Brain

11 Saw two trapezoidal support pads 3.5 mm x 6 mm from the same sterling silver sheet. Use cut-and-slot construction to fit them to the studs. (See Diagram H on page 98.)

12 Set up and solder the pads onto the studs. (See Diagram I on page 98.)

13 Place a brass brush in the flex-shaft and, WEARING GOGGLES or a FACE SHIELD, dip the stationary wheel into soapy water to lubricate it. Running at a very slow speed, brush all rear surfaces, re-wetting the wheel often.

14 Determine the locations of the pin joint and catch on the two pads. Solder the joint first, then the catch. Pickle and brass-brush again.

15 Blacken the silver by dipping it into a warm, diluted solution of liver-of-sulfur and water with a drop of ammonia.

16 Remove discoloration from the silver back surfaces with a brass brush. Use a polished steel burnisher to rub and "brighten" the edges.

17 Set the stones by pushing the soft 24k gold over the perimeter.

18 Cut the pin stem to length; file and polish the tip. Insert it into the joint and secure with a rivet.

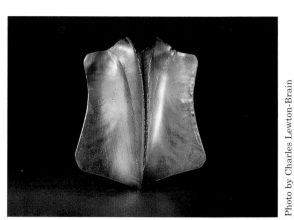

Swoop Series Brooch

Photo by Charles Lewton-Brain

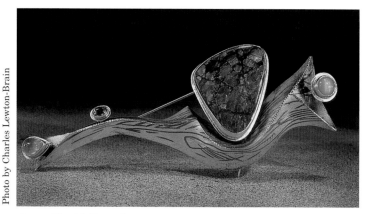

Ammolite #2 Brooch

Photo by Charles Lewton-Brain

Field Brooch

Photo by Charles Lewton-Brain

LOES VAN RIEL

"I was never supposed to be an artist," says Loes van Riel. But growing up in a family where everyone has artistic leanings makes it hard to fully escape. "My father designed store windows; one brother is a photographer; one runs a jazz club; and another works in illuminated advertising. My mother was a late bloomer, who came to painting in the middle of her life and then went on to show in exhibitions. I guess it is in my genes." Loes was virtually pulled into the arts whether she liked it or not.

Square Grafika Earrings

Photo by Ralph Gabriner

Loes van Riel grew up in Amsterdam, the Netherlands, where she says, "I was raised to be, well, a girl." Being a wife and mother was the plan, and that is exactly what she intended to do. Having her own career was never really an option. After she finished school, her suppressed adventurous streak struck and she came to America to work as a nanny, a position that was supposed to last one year. But at the end of the year, Loes decided that she wanted to stay. Uncertain where her calling lay, she tried several jobs, but nothing grabbed her as the "right" career.

In the meantime, she did a stint in college and married American, Robert Pfuelb, an up-and-coming jewelry artist. When his business grew, she joined up and took over the unpopular tasks of keeping the books, paying the bills, doing the shipping, etc. She helped him at craft shows, hardly paying attention to the way jewelry was made. And then, one morning, she awoke from a dream that changed her life. Vivid images of a different kind of jewelry filled her head and she nearly burst with excitement to bring these images to life. When she described them to Bob and suggested that he make them, he told her that if she wanted her ideas created her way; she would have to do it herself. And so she did.

Although she had no formal training in jewelry, she had picked up quite a bit by just being around it. That, along with her hidden artistic talent, propelled Loes to explore and develop an incredible collection of very unique jewelry. "I was exposed to a few different materials, but when I came to gold leaf, I fell in love," Loes glows. "22k gold has a luminosity and presence unlike anything else, and it fits in with the graphic qualities of my images." Loes has found herself in the unusual niche that brings jewelry, papermaking, and graphic design together with old images from her life.

Photo by Robert Pfuelb

ANNE FRANK BROOCH

Photo by Ralph Gabriner

Growing up in Amsterdam, Loes was very aware of the Anne Frank story. Her attempt to combine that theme with her contemporary jewelry was an unexpected and overwhelming success. Originally intended as a one-of-a-kind piece, this brooch has touched countless people. Loes has reproduced it for hundreds of individuals and groups.

ANNE FRANK BROOCH

Materials

		Measurements
	Sterling silver sheet	0.8 mm (20 gauge); 0.6 mm (22 gauge)
	Postage stamp	
	Adhesive letters	
22k	Gold leaf	
	Sterling silver ear posts	0.9 mm diameter with 1.5 mm pads - 5 pieces
	Sterling silver pin findings	

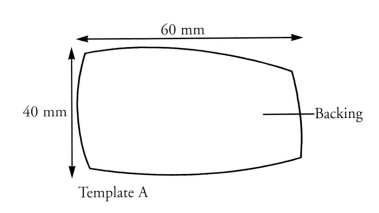

Template A

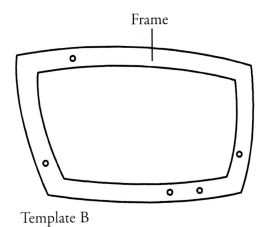

Frame

Template B

Diagram A

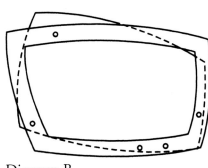

Diagram B

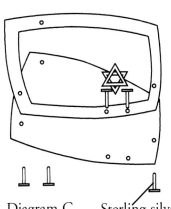

Diagram C

Sterling silver
ear posts as
rivets

ANNE FRANK BROOCH

1 Lightly coat the silver sheet for the backing and frame with white watercolor paint. (See Templates A and B on page 103.) Place Template A and B on 0.8 mm and 0.6 mm sterling silver sheet respectively. Transfer the patterns with carbon paper. Use a jeweler's saw to cut out the pieces and dome them slightly over a large round stake so that they fit together.

2 Cut two equilateral triangles, 11 mm per side, from 0.6 mm sterling silver sheet. (See Diagram A on page 103.) Drill a hole and pierce the centers, leaving 3 mm wide edges. Sand the pieces smooth and solder them together to form a Star of David. Solder two sterling silver ear posts with pads (available commercially) to the back of the star for use as rivets. (See Diagram C on page 103.)

3 Tape the backing and frame together. Mark the points where the star's posts will be located. Mark locations for the other three rivets that will hold the assembly together. Drill five 0.9 mm holes through both the backing and frame, making certain that the holes line up perfectly. (See Template B on page 103.) Use a round bur to countersink (or chamfer) each hole on the front of the frame and on the back of the backing piece.

4 Solder a pin catch and joint to the rear of the backing, approximately 6 mm from the top.

5 Clean and polish all pieces, using an abrasive pad to impart a soft, brushed texture.

6 Apply a collage, using a postage stamp and 22k gold leaf. Use shoemaker's glue as the adhesive. (Detailed instructions can be found in craft books.) Apply gold leaf by painting

Zandvoort Brooch

Photo by Ralph Gabriner

De Koffers Brooch

Photo by Ralph Gabriner

104

a layer of quick-size on the surface. Let dry for about three hours to just barely tacky. Apply gold leaf and let dry for twenty-four hours. Burnish lightly with a cotton ball. Add adhesive letters after the gold leaf is burnished.

7 After the collage is completely dry, apply a very thin coat of clear spray lacquer. Wait an hour and then apply another seven thin coats and continue at the rate of one per hour, no faster. Allow the lacquer to cure for at least five days. *Note: Spray lacquer is toxic. Take appropriate precautions against inhalation.*

8 Assemble the backing and frame. Using transparent tape to hold the parts together, place three rivets through the holes from the back. Cut each rivet so that approximately 1 mm protrudes on the front. (See Diagram C on page 103.)

9 Place the work over a steel block, with a couple of sheets of tracing paper to prevent marring the surfaces. Use a ball-peen hammer to "upset" or flare the rivets neatly and evenly.

10 Insert the star rivets into the holes from the front and upset the rivets on the back. Attach the pin stem to the joint.

Arched Grafika Earrings

Photo by Ralph Gabriner

Kabuki Brooch

Photo by Ralph Gabriner

NEAL POLLACK

Neal Pollack was honorably discharged from the United States Army on April 17, 1969, after serving a two-year tour in Viet Nam. Prior to his induction, he had long hair, tight pants, and was playing electric bass in a blues/rock band in Chicago. When he returned home, Neal realized that the skills he had most recently acquired would be of very little use to him now, so he drove a taxicab while trying to decide what to do with the rest of his life. An old friend and goldsmith, Marvin Berkman, had just opened a "hand-made jewelry" shop in the historic Old Town district. When Neal went to visit, he was transfixed, watching the master solder a silver ring together. "It was the closest thing to magic I had ever seen and I was hooked!" Neal says. When he asked his friend to teach him, Marvin just pointed to a chair and said, "Sit down." That was the first day of a four-year apprenticeship, during which Neal learned all phases of making jewelry.

After his apprenticeship, Neal moved to Pforzheim, Germany, a town so dominated by jewelry that it is called "The Gold City." Neal attended the respected goldsmithing school and supported himself by doing production work at one of the city's hundreds of jewelry manufacturers. Returning to the US with European skills and six years of experience, Neal opened his own shop on Chicago's North Shore. For the next 13 years, he made custom jewelry for the upscale local clientele. "I wanted to revive a pride in workmanship and an integrity of design," Neal recalls.

Split Leaf Necklace

Photo by Neal Pollack

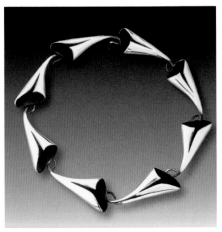

Pod Choker

Photo by Neal Pollack

Photo by Jean Dupré

While vacationing in Colorado, Neal realized that he preferred mountains to concrete; and in 1987 he set up a small custom jewelry studio in the Aspen area. Pollack lives nearby with his wife Jean Dupré, on 11 acres beside a trout stream. "When I returned from Viet Nam, all I wanted was a beautiful wife, a place in the country, interesting work, and a car that was paid for. I have all that and more. It amazes me that after all these years, I still feel the same magic every time I sit down at the bench. I am the luckiest man in the world."

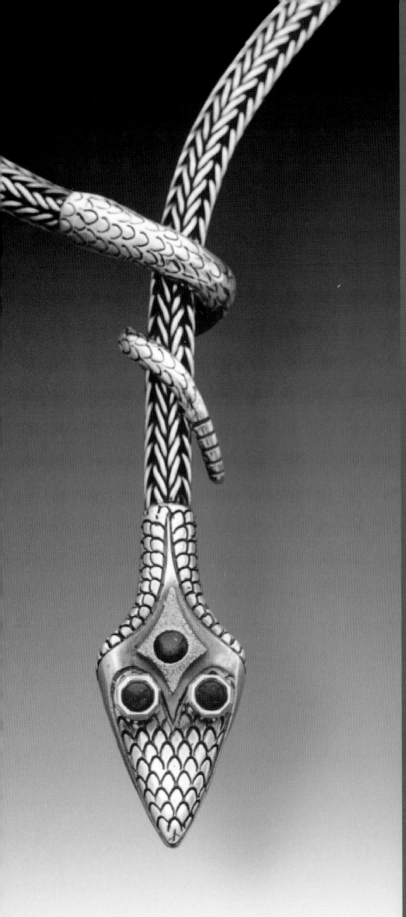

Photo by Neal Pollack

SNAKE NECKLACE

I wanted to take advantage of this chain's 'snaky' quality to create a flexible, whimsical necklace with an integrated lock that had no moving pieces," says the artist. "Interestingly enough, this piece was purchased by a woman who was afraid of snakes."

SNAKE NECKLACE

Materials		*Measurements*
	Sterling silver casting shot	
	Sterling silver wire	0.9 mm (19 gauge) x about 20 meters (60 feet)
14k	Yellow gold sheet	1 mm (18 gauge)
14k	Yellow gold rod	3 mm diameter
	Black star sapphire	4 mm round
	Green opals	5 mm round - 2 pieces
14k	Yellow gold tubing	5 mm outside diameter
	Carving wax	

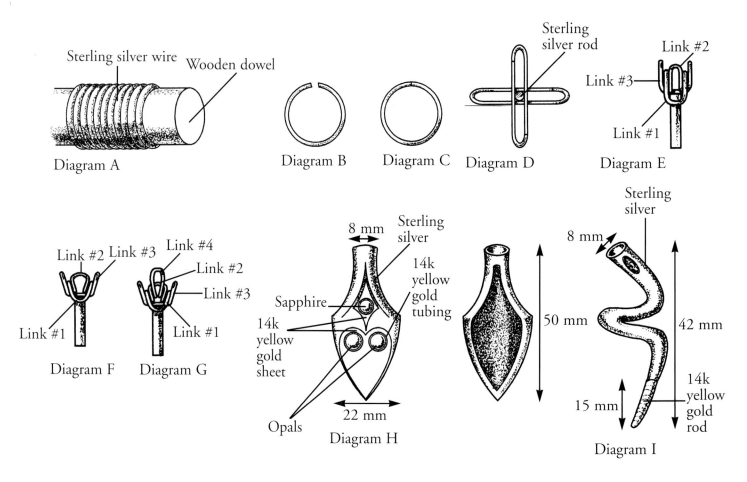

Diagram A

Diagram B

Diagram C

Diagram D

Diagram E

Diagram F

Diagram G

Diagram H

Diagram I

SNAKE NECKLACE

1   Cut the sterling silver wire into four equal pieces for ease of handling. Wrap the wire around a wooden dowel 12.75 mm in diameter. (See Diagram A on page 108.)

2   Mark a straight line down the tightly wrapped coil and use flush cutting pliers to clip equal-sized jump rings. (See Diagram B on page 108.) Align the ends and join with hard solder. (Diagram C on page 108.)

3   Use either pliers or hooks to stretch the rings into elongated loops. Solder two loops together around a 1.5 mm sterling silver rod to create a handle and starting point. (See Diagram D on page 108.)

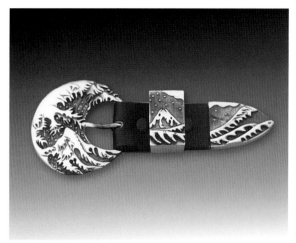

Wave Ranger Set

Photo by Neal Pollack

4   Bend up the bottom link, forming a "U". Bend up the next link in the same manner. Insert the third link into the first, bend it into a "U". (See Diagram E on page 108 .)

5   Push the third link down and use a long, gently tapered awl to poke through to enlarge the hole in link #2 for the next link. (See Diagram F on page 108.) Insert the fourth link into the second and bend it up. (See Diagram G on page 108.) *Note: Odd-numbered links cross even-numbered links.*

6   Push the third link down so it fits tightly into the first, and insert link number 5 through 3 and 1 and bend it up. Repeat with number 6, going through 4 and 2, etc. Continue to add links until the chain is complete with about 320 links and about 50 cm long. Anneal the completed chain.

7   At this point, the chain shows some irregularities from hand assembly. The appearance can be improved by gently tapping the chain with a large mallet, or by drawing the chain through a draw plate. Steel draw plates work well, although they tend to leave a small flat spot on the outer edge of each link. A wooden draw plate, which does not distort the chain, can be made by drilling a piece of hardwood, about 12.5 mm thick, with three drill bits—8 mm, 7.5 mm, and 7 mm.

8   Lubricate the chain with soap and draw it down to a uniform thickness. It stretches out a bit to approximately 60 cm long. Drawing the chain further will compress it and tighten the movement.

9   Carve the head and tail from wax to the dimensions given. Carve openings for the chain in the head and tail. The head is further hollowed to lighten it. Carve scales into the pieces either with a graver, or a scribe. (See Diagram H on page 108.)

10 Cast the two pieces in sterling silver and finish them.

11 Solder a piece of 3 mm gold rod to the tail with silver hard solder. File it to a taper. Carve the rings with needle files. (See Diagram I on page 108.)

12 Cut a piece of gold sheet for the diamond-shaped section on the head. Cut two sections of 5 mm gold tubing as bezels for the opals. Solder these, along with diamond-shaped piece, onto the head with silver hard solder.

13 Insert the chain into the tail and head. Join the components with silver medium solder by flowing solder first into the openings in the silver sections, then pushing the chain into place and reheating to sweat-solder the chain at all the contact points.

14 Apply liver-of-sulfur or another agent to the entire piece to blacken it. Polish the high points with rouge. Rinse and remove all compound.

15 Drill the plate for the central star sapphire and use a bur to create a seat. Place the stone in position, then push the surrounding metal over it with a hammer and punch. Mask the marks with a stippled texture made with a hammer and center punch.

16 Place the opals into the bezels and push the metal over with a setting pusher or punch. File the perimeter to a hexagonal shape. Touch up the settings with rouge as necessary.

Panther Cuff

Photo by Neal Pollack

Panther Cuff

Photo by Neal Pollack

Australopithecus Robustus

Photo by Neal Pollack

PAUL ROBILOTTI

Photo by Ralph Gabriner

Edera Brooch

The son of an architect, Paul Robilotti was drawn to classical design, especially ancient Greek and Roman architecture, from an early age. At the age of nine, he began taking classes at the Roberson Center for the Arts and Sciences, near his home in upstate New York. "When I was 12, I took my first jewelry class," Paul remembers. "It was a great match from the start. Growing up in an atmosphere where form, structure, and texture were tangible concepts, this new-found medium was perfect for me to express my ideas."

By the time he reached high school, Paul was designing for a national chain of jewelry stores, where his creations were displayed side-by-side with major manufacturers. Knowing that he had a lot more to learn, after high school Paul enrolled at New York's Fashion Institute of Technology, where he was able to study with some of the industry's top designers and craftsmen. "New York was very stimulating for me. An entire universe awaited my discovery! Tools, teachers, and libraries of information were all at my fingertips."

After working as a model maker for several big-name designers, Paul broke out on his own, creating a collection with a classical/architectural slant. Paul's jewelry has gained wide recognition within the jewelry industry and beyond, as awards continue to mount up from DeBeers (the world's major diamond producer), JCK magazine, Modern Jeweler, etc.

Paul's work represents a life-long fascination with the balance and symmetry that links art and architecture over the millennia. For Paul, the task has always been to examine the classics and distill the components of proportion, drama, and form to the point where he fully understands them. Once

ROBILOTTI

integrated, these timeless qualities become the language for Paul's interpretation and artistic expression in contemporary jewelry. Paul's 18k gold and platinum jewelry, accented by rubies, pearls, and diamonds, would equally enhance the wardrobe of an elegant Venetian princess, a wild Hollywood flapper, or a sophisticated cyber star in the year 2000. Simply stated, Paul Robilotti carves out his future by reflecting on the past.

Photo by J. Robilotti

Greco Men's Ring

EDERA EARRINGS

Photo by Ralph Gabriner

The motif for these earrings is based on an intricate architectural frieze on a building in Florence, Italy. Sketches are made, then models are carved in wax and then cast, followed by the assemblage of the components.

EDERA EARRINGS

Materials		Measurements
	Carving wax	5 mm thick
18k	Yellow gold casting shot	
18k	Yellow gold sheet	0.5 mm
18k	Yellow gold round wire	2 mm; 1.2 mm; 0.9 mm; 0.8 mm
18k	Yellow gold omega earring backs	
	Triangle-shaped blister pearls	18 mm

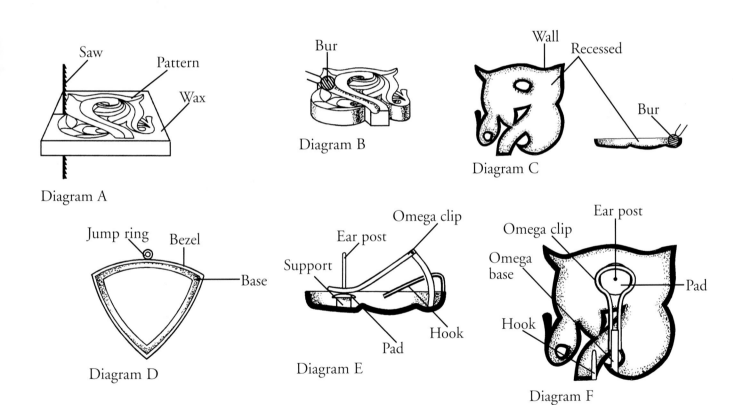

Diagram A

Diagram B

Diagram C

Diagram D

Diagram E

Diagram F

EDERA EARRINGS

1 Glue mirror images of the design onto a block of hard wax. Transfer the patterns by poking holes along each line. Remove the paper and connect the dots with a permanent marker. Use a jeweler's saw to follow each perimeter and then file the sides perpendicular to the top.

2 Drill holes and use a saw to pierce the interior spaces. Glue the two earring models together, back to back, aligned perfectly. Correct the outlines. (See Diagram A on page 113.)

3 Use a marker to indicate the relief, showing the high and low areas. Carve the relief with burs, knives, scrapers, gravers, and files, whatever tools work best. Use a scraper or sandpaper to finish the fronts. Burnish the surfaces with a coarse cloth, or use a solvent like benzene (SAFETY HAZARD) on a cotton swab, or use your torch (EXPERTS ONLY) to "flame polish" the waxes. (See Diagram B on page 113.)

4 Separate the halves and scribe a line 1.5 mm inside the perimeter on the back of each. Use coarse burs to remove wax from the backs, leaving the 1.5 mm wall around the outside and a thickness of about 0.6 mm elsewhere. Use a spring gauge to check the thickness. (See Diagram C on page 113.)

5 Carve a shallow relief onto two 8 mm diameter wax discs as pads for the ear posts.

6 Add sprues to all four parts and cast as separate units, so that the pads and earrings can be polished separately before assembly. After casting, clip or saw the sprues and bring the surface to a very fine finish with files, abrasive papers, and rubberized abrasive wheels.

Renaissance Brooch

Photo by Judy Robilotti

7 Cut two 4 mm wide strips from 0.5 mm gold sheet for the bezels. Use a combination of pliers and your fingers to shape them to the contours of the pearls. Trim and join the ends with gold hard solder. Add 0.5 mm thick base to each with gold medium solder. Saw and file the edges flush and polish. (See Diagram D on page 113.)

8 Wrap 0.8 mm gold round wire around a 1.5 mm spindle for the jump rings. Saw off two rings, align the ends and place the seam of each against a bezel. Secure with 18k yellow gold easy solder.

9 Cut off two supports for the ear pads from 2 mm gold round wire. Adjust the lengths so that the pads sit about 0.5 mm below the back plane of each earring, at about ⅓ of the way from the top. Use gold hard solder to join the supports to the earrings and to add the pads. Drill a 0.9 mm hole about 1 mm deep into the center of each pad and use gold medium solder to secure a 0.9 mm thick gold round wire post, 12 mm long to each. (See Diagram E and F on page 113.)

10 Omega clips, either purchased or fabricated, are added on the back of each earring for security and comfort. Remove the rivet and disassemble the Omega's clip and base. Use gold medium solder to secure the Omega's base, positioned so that clip closes over the post. Cut two pieces of 1.2 mm gold round wire, 15 mm long for hooks to hold the pearl drops. Shape the hooks to follow the contour of the back of each earring, with the first 3 mm perpendicular. Secure with gold easy solder. Reassemble the Omega and upset the rivets.

11 Add a dramatic contrast and evoke a soft sensual quality by sandblasting the front surfaces. Use rubber abrasive wheels to highlight the raised edges, leaving a high polish.

12 Set the pearls to complete the earrings.

Photo by J. Robilotti

Renaissance Necklace

Photo by Ralph Gabriner

Edera Necklace

ROBERT PFUELB

Photo by Ralph Gabriner

Lentil / Wand Necklace

As if predestined for the life of an artist, the only subject Robert Pfuelb actually enjoyed in school was art. His preoccupation with this one subject was a cause of great concern in the Pfuelb family. Much to his parent's dismay, their son's favorite toys were not baseball bats and toy guns, but the hand tools he found in his father's tool cabinet. In school, as at home, no one knew quite what to do with Bob. Almost oblivious to the consternation he caused in those around him, Bob was happily following his own path, ignoring the distractions of school, TV, sports, etc., in favor of working with his hands, creating art. Looking back, he says, "I have always seen myself as an artist, and never imagined doing anything else."

Photo by Loes van Riel

While the rest gave up hope, one high school teacher noticed this talented and motivated young man in his classes—the art teacher. "It was clear to everyone that rocket science would have to develop without me," Robert recalls. "I felt a calling to the arts and luckily found a few nurturing teachers along the way, who fed my interest."

After receiving his Bachelor's degree in Art Education, Bob began teaching high school art. When the principal asked if he could add a class in jewelry, Bob confidently agreed even though he had never touched metal. To his great surprise, however, not only was he able to master the basics enough to lead the class in jewelry making, but he also discovered that he liked it. "After all," he told himself, "design is design. I can just as easily express my ideas in silver and gold as I can using acrylics on canvas."

Bob dreamed of living and working in Europe. Since his former wife Loes came from Amsterdam, they decided to relocate in the Netherlands. Bob lived out that dream, painting and making jewelry in one of the world's most important art centers. In 1974 he returned to the States and resumed teaching and making jewelry. He started selling at craft shows in the early eighties, just in time to prevent a major meltdown from teacher burnout. When he finally retired from teaching, he literally tap-danced his way down the hall and out the door.

Bob has continued to focus on jewelry, never ceasing to come up with new ideas, seemingly out of the blue. For Robert Pfuelb, jewelry is a complete and compelling art that continues to satisfy him. "I am forever drawn in by the medium," he says. "Working with tools, metals, and gems pulls me back to my bench day after day after day, without ever being bored."

This is an example of a very simple linkage system used to create an elegant and flexible necklace. The entire piece is made from nearly identical links cut from gold sheet, plus a bezel and clasp. A bead blaster (like a sand blaster but emitting larger polished glass beads) is used to create a soft texture, adding dramatic contrast to the polished surfaces.

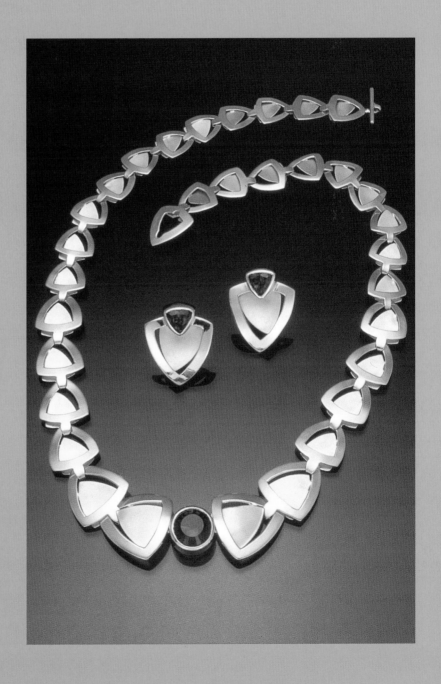

MULTI–LINK RHODALITE NECKLACE

Materials

		Measurements
18k	Yellow gold sheet (annealed)	0.6 mm (22 gauge); 0.5 mm (24 gauge)
18k	Yellow gold wire	1.3 mm (16 gauge)
	Rhodalite	9 mm

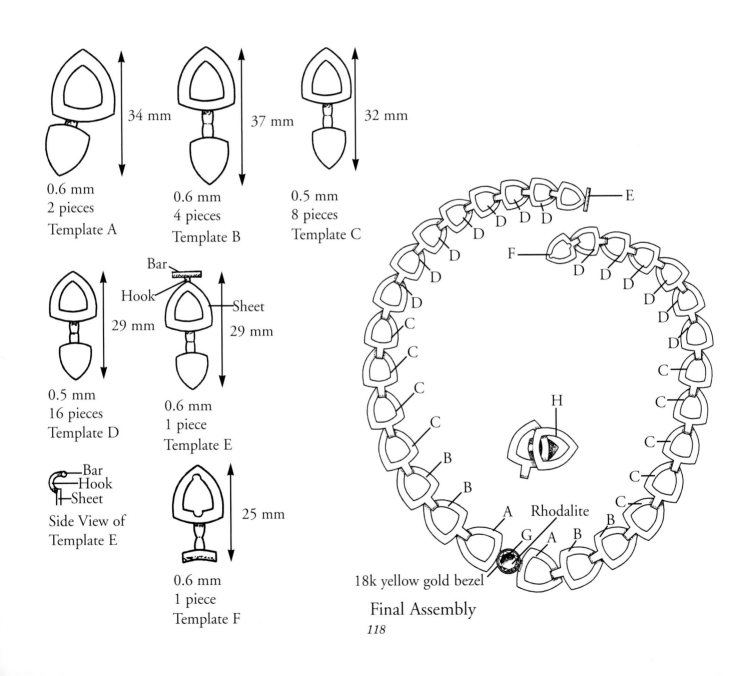

34 mm

0.6 mm
2 pieces
Template A

37 mm

0.6 mm
4 pieces
Template B

32 mm

0.5 mm
8 pieces
Template C

Bar
Hook

29 mm

0.5 mm
16 pieces
Template D

Hook
Sheet

29 mm

0.6 mm
1 piece
Template E

Bar
Hook
Sheet

Side View of
Template E

25 mm

0.6 mm
1 piece
Template F

E
D D D
F
D
D
D
D
D
D
D
C
C
C
C
C
C
C
C
B
B
B
B
A
G A
Rhodalite
H

18k yellow gold bezel

Final Assembly

118

MULTI-LINK RHODALITE NECKLACE

1   Make a bezel for the 9 mm stone by cutting a rectangle of 0.5 mm gold sheet 30 mm x about 9 mm (depending on the height of the stone). Roll the piece into a cylinder around the shaft of a dapping punch; adjust the fit and solder closed. This bezel should fit around the stone. If necessary, make further adjustments.

2   Make a seat for the bezel from a rectangle of 0.5 mm gold sheet cut to 26.7 mm x 7 mm (again depending on the stone). Form this into a cylinder as above, which should fit snugly inside the larger, providing a seat for the stone to rest on. Solder the two cylinders together, one inside the other, with the bottoms flush.

3   (See Templates A–D on page 118.) Use Templates A–D to cut 30 links, adjusting the number for the length you need, in the four template sizes, from 0.6 gold sheet. Be certain that the small solid triangle of each link slips through the hole of the adjoining link. File the edges as necessary.

4   Place each link into a large (65 mm) depression and use a dapping punch, slightly smaller than the hole, to shape them and add dimension. The two largest links (Template A) are dapped from opposite sides to create mirror images of each other. Clean up and polish the links. For added contrast, bead blast (or use another texture) on the concave side of each link.

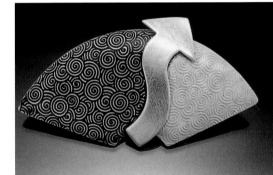

Fan Arrow Brooch

Photo by Ralph Gabriner

5   Fold the largest links over at the tabs so that they are asymmetrical and mirror images of each other, with each tip of the small triangle poking out through the hole. Shift each tip to the side to leave room for the tab of the next link.

6   Set up and solder the two largest links to the bezel at mirror image angles just above the midpoint in the bezel to follow the natural curve of the necklace. (See Final Assembly G on page 118.)

7   Bend the remainder of the links around a 2.4 mm shaft (a standard bur shaft works) so the tab has a rounded shape. This is essential for smooth movement when the links are strung together.

8 Thread the second link (Template B) through the hole in the first link (Template A) and push the small triangle to one side (for example, to the left on pieces left of the bezel and to the right on the other side). Secure the link by tacking it at the contact point of the small gold triangle and the large triangular hole with solder. Repeat the process, working symmetrically on both sides to insure uniformity, until all but the two end links are added. (See Final Assembly H on page 118.)

9 Make the bar and hook from two 12 mm pieces of 1.3 mm gold round wire. Bend one piece into a "U", with one side a little bit longer than the other. (See View of Template E on page 118.) Solder the short side to the middle of the other wire with gold hard solder. Attach this hook to the end of the last link on one side, before attaching the link to the necklace.

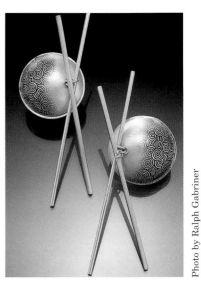

Photo by Ralph Gabriner

Photo by Ralph Gabriner

10 Carve two grooves into the last mating link for the other side. Add the two last links and secure them as before, by tacking them at the contact points. (See Final Assembly F on page 118.) Because the hook will enter and engage this link, a bar replaces the triangle on the back.

11 Finish the entire necklace by buffing and polishing as necessary.

Charm Necklace   *XO Earrings*

12 Insert the stone. Check the fit and adjust as necessary. If the stone sits too high, use a setting bur to bevel the top of the seat so that it matches the angle of the pavilion and lets the stone drop in further. The bezel should cover about ⅓ of the crown.

13 Close the bezel over the stone with a bezel roller or with a punch and hammer. Clean the bezel with a pumice wheel and polish. *Note: Often, the necklace is adjusted so the links lie flat and sit comfortably on the wearer.*

MICHAEL GOOD

Born in the U.S. of Belgian parents, Michael Good spent most of his youth on the East coast, while summers were spent with family in Europe. "I remember trying to conform to the society around me, which I neither understood nor believed in," he recalls.

After a year of college, Michael dropped out to help establish a school for delinquent children on New York's Lower East Side. Eight years later, when he realized he could not change the world, Michael and his wife Karen left the hustle and bustle of city life for the serenity of country life. In a desperate attempt to gain skills which could provide a living for his family, Michael learned the basics of making jewelry before he and his family moved to a small village on the Maine coast.

Photo by Carol Miller

Double Loop Bracelet

Looking through a German magazine, Michael discovered the work of Friedrich Becker, a contemporary German jeweler with an aerospace engineering background. "His work defied all that I had known about jewelry before. It was sleek and elegant and it was made up of smoothly flowing kinetic elements. It dawned on me that there was more to jewelry than I had been told," says the artist. "From that point onward, jewelry took on a new meaning for me. It became a vehicle for my investigation of both technical and philosophical concepts with a far deeper meaning than mere personal adornment."

On his own, without a teacher, Michael decided to explore the medium from a new perspective. He took on the goal of creating hollow-formed jewelry with the maximum volume and structural integrity, using the least amount of material. At around this same time, Micheal was introduced to anticlastic raising, an approach developed by Heikki Seppa. This revolutionary system of metalsmithing provides a method for creating curvilinear tubes of varying diameters, and then builds an encyclopedia of new forms around it. Integrating

Photo by Avi Good

this technique with his own, Micheal began to create jewelry like no one else's.

Michael's work raised jewelry to a new level of elegance and simplicity. Now, over 20 years later, Michael's sensuous forms in gold and platinum have earned him an international reputation. His jewelry is sold at the finest jewelry stores and galleries in North America, Europe, and Japan. Truly, the path through jewelry can lead almost anywhere. The only limitations are the dedication, innovation, and imagination of the maker.

Photo by Bill Thuss

OPEN SEAM BRACELET

This basic project demonstrates the malleability of metal as well as the principles of anticlastic raising. Understanding some of the special terminology used to describe this system of forming metal sheet helps clarify the process. "Anticlastic forms" have two curved axes opposing each other at 90°, similar to the shape of a saddle. The "generator" curve follows the back of the horse and describes the overall shape of the piece. The "axial" curve fits the rider and describes the internal diameter within the actual piece. These two curves are interdependent so that when you close one the effect is to open the other, unless force is exerted to keep the second curve from expanding. The process is simple in theory and utilizes a specialized "sinusoidal" stake, which can be purchased from some suppliers or carved from hard plastic, wood, or steel. The dimensions of the stake determine the limits to which a piece of sheet can be formed. The thickness of the stake determines the minimum "axial" curve of the final form. The distance between the crests determines the maximum "generator curve," the diameter of the finished piece. When completed, this bracelet is left with an open seam which makes it flexible to sideways twisting, so that the wrist can be inserted.

OPEN SEAM BRACELET

Materials

Measurements

18k   Yellow gold sheet   0.5 mm (24 gauge) x 180 mm long

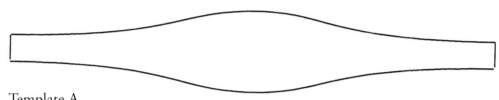

Template A

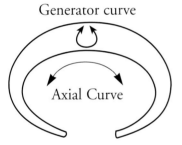

Generator curve

Axial Curve

Anticlastic Terminology

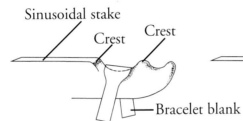

Sinusoidal stake

Crest   Crest

Bracelet blank

Diagram A

Cross peen hammer

Diagram B

Diagram C

Diagram D

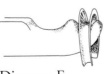

Diagram E

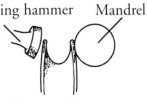

Planishing hammer   Mandrel

Diagram F

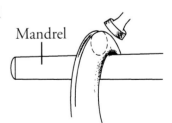

Mandrel

Diagram G

Diagram H

Diagram I

Diagram J

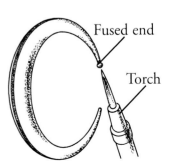

Fused end

Torch

Diagram K

OPEN SEAM BRACELET

1 Use shears to cut out the bracelet blank from 0.5 mm gold sheet. (See Template A on page 123.) File the edges and anneal the metal.

Figure 8

Photo by Jeff Slack

2 Mount a sinusoidal stake securely in a bench vise. Bend the blank over the stake into a "U" which will be the beginning of the axial curve. The width of the sheet should not exceed the distance between two crests of the stake. (See Diagram A on page 123.) Holding both sides of the sheet firmly in place, use a cross-peen hammer to strike the metal just below the point where it meets the stake. *Note: The hammer and stake should be made of different materials. If the stake is plastic, use a steel hammer. If the stake is steel, use a plastic hammer.* By holding the sides of the blank firmly against the force, they exert outward, the anticlastic form develops with each hammer blow. As the edge of the metal curls inward, the generator curve develops. (See Diagram B on page 123.)

3 Slide the sheet along as the hammer continues to strike the edge in overlapping blows, curling more and more of the metal into a smooth and even furrow. Turn the metal around 180° so that the other edge of the metal is in position to strike and repeat the process; hold the metal firmly, striking it below the edge in overlapping blows. (See Diagram C on page 123.)

4 Repeat Steps 2–3, this time striking the sheet a little lower, or closer to the middle, between the bottom of the furrow you just made and the middle of the blank, making the furrow wider. (See Diagram D on page 123.) Flip the piece around again and repeat on the other side. The effect is to reduce the ridge between the furrows in the middle of the form. Repeat as the ridge in the middle becomes even narrower. (See Diagram D on page 123.)

5 Repeating again, force the ridge into the stake, creating a smooth generator curve. This completes the first course. Anneal the metal. (See Diagram D on page 123.)

6 Before beginning the second course, use your hands to force the ends of the blank together, tightening the axial curve, and thereby opening the generator curve so that once again the edges of the metal rest inside the crests of the stake. If the limits of the first curve in the stake have been reached, move the metal down to the next smaller groove in the stake. In most cases, two courses in the first groove are necessary.

Photo by TPS Visual

Spirit Sun Pendant with Spirit Sun® Diamond

7 Continue the anticlastic process until the sides are raised enough so that the desired axial and generator curves are smooth and form part of a perfect oval in cross section. (See Diagram E on page 123.)

8 Close the form into a tube by removing the sinusoidal stake and mounting a smooth tapered mandrel, such as a ring mandrel, in the vise. Hold the metal against the mandrel, and strike the side with a planishing hammer to close in the sides. Alternate hammering one side evenly from one end to the other and then flip the metal and work on the other side. (See Diagram F on page 123.)

9 When the edges approach each other, reposition the work so that it is supported from inside the axial curve. (See Diagram G on page 123.) Hammer the edges inward as the tube bulges out into a round cross section. (See Diagram H on page 123.) Alternate striking one edge and then the other until they meet. (See Diagram I on page 123.)

10 The form is complete when there is a narrow and evenly spaced gap between the edges. (See Diagram J on page 123.) The seam is left open and unsoldered. This provides a natural resilience so that the metal will flex and return to its proper position. If soldered, the metal would become rigid. When executed properly, only a minimum of filing and sanding are required to finish the surface.

11 Complete the ends of the bracelet by fusing them into equal-sized balls. (See Diagram K on page 123.) Clean and flux the ends, then direct the torch to melt the extremities evenly. This definitely takes practice, and since it is an irreversible process, practice on scrap first.

12 Repolish as necessary and give the bracelet a slight sideways twist so that the ends are offset. Because the seam has been left open, the wearer can spring the ends slightly further offset in order to slip it on the wrist. The springy metal returns to its correct shape without permanent distortion.

JAN MADDOX

Photo by Jerry Maddox

When Jan Maddox entered the University of Nebraska in 1949, she declared as an art major, taking the usual classes in painting, drawing, etc. When an evening class was offered in jewelry making, she signed up out of curiosity. The class changed her life. This was an exciting new world full of tools, terms, and techniques Jan had never heard of, and the possibilities were limitless. "The workshop was minimal. We only had a few simple tools, but that didn't stop us," recalls Jan. "I learned to solder, using a blowpipe and we enameled over a Bunsen burner. It wasn't fancy, but it worked!" The year was 1952 and within 12 months she took part in her first jewelry exhibition. Jan had little idea she would soon join a small but growing group of America's artist/jewelers.

Jan finished with a Bachelor of Fine Arts degree and later went to Indiana University for graduate school. Jan was now certain of her direction, "Jewelry fascinated me more and more. I felt drawn to it. I felt there was a lot to explore in it."

Out on her own, Jan used a basic set of hand tools to turn some scrap silver into pieces for a local craft show, where she found a ready market for her work. And, from that point onward, Jan's career paralleled the course of the American jewelry renaissance which was part of the rapidly growing crafts movement. Jewelry was exactly where Jan wanted to be and her work was immediately recognized for its artistry. She exhibited in the seminal "Young Americans, 1962," at the Museum of Contemporary Crafts in New York.

In 1971 Jan was offered a full-time teaching position at Montgomery College in Rockville, Maryland. Over the next 25 years she taught jewelry making as well as general crafts, two- and three-dimensional design, ceramics, and art appreciation. Eventually Jan became a full professor, but she never stopped producing her own work.

As Jan's teaching career evolved and matured, so did her own artistry. A committed explorer, Jan has pursued a variety of styles and media, both precious and non-precious, always imparting her own vocabulary of simple, sometimes geometric shapes. "I love the feel of metal, especially sterling silver. I am forever fascinated by the process of building things," says Jan. But her enjoyment does not stop there. "I also like to sell my work as the final step in the cycle. I begin with raw materials and through my efforts they end up as someone else's treasure." Looking back at over 45 years in the crafts movement, Jan reflects with typical modesty saying, "I may not have produced a great quantity of work, but when you add family, teaching, community, personal discovery, and technical exploration, I feel I have had a rich, full life—at least so far."

Photo by Jerry Maddox

Bigger Book

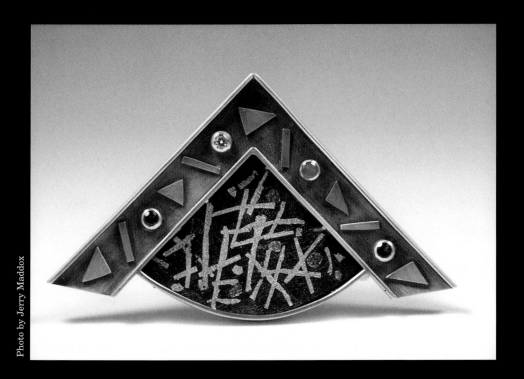

Photo by Jerry Maddox

Damascene is an inclusive term referring to the inlay of one metal into another. Variations on the technique occur in many Middle Eastern and Asian cultures. In Japan the technique is called "nunome zogan" meaning cloth inlay, a reference to the weave-like cross hatching made in the steel prior to inlay. Jan's interpretation, as might be predicted, does not limit itself to traditional boundaries. In this innovative brooch, she applies 24k gold as well as ordinary colored florist's foils onto the steel surface.

QUARTER CIRCLE PIN WITH DAMASCENE INLAY

Materials		*Measurements*
	Sterling silver sheet:	1 mm (18 gauge); 0.8 mm (20 gauge); 0.5 mm (24 gauge)
18k	Yellow gold/sterling silver bimetal	0.5 mm (24 gauge)
	Sterling silver tubing	4 mm outside diameter
	Amethyst, emerald, garnet and CZ	3.5 mm diameter - 1 piece of each
	Mild steel for damascene	1 mm (18 gauge)
24k	Gold foil (enamelists foil or thicker, NOT gold leaf)	
	Thick florists foils in red and green	
	Sterling silver pin findings	
	Nickel silver pin stem	

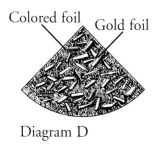

Cross hatched mild steel

Diagram A

Silver sheet   90° Crease

Diagram B

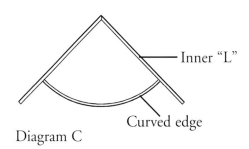

Inner "L"

Curved edge

Diagram C

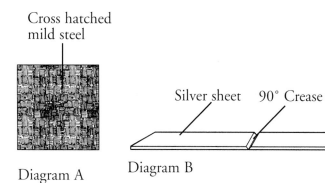

Colored foil   Gold foil

Diagram D

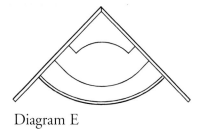

Diagram E

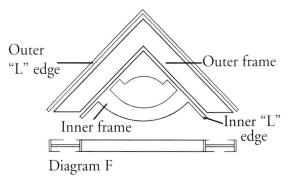

Outer "L" edge   Outer frame

Inner frame   Inner "L" edge

Diagram F

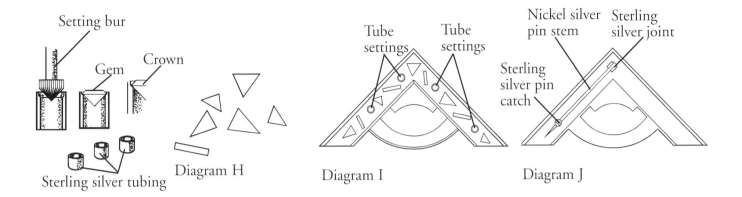

Diagram G

QUARTER CIRCLE PIN WITH DAMASCENE INLAY

1 Prepare a piece of mild steel for damascene inlay. Use a sharp, fairly wide steel punch to stamp lines closely together across the entire surface. Stamp an area larger than needed and repeat the pattern in the three other directions so that lines run vertically and horizontally as well as diagonally between pairs of opposite corners. This creates a rough surface of steel points to grip the foil as it is applied. (See Diagram A on page 128.)

2 Cut off about 100 mm of 1 mm x 6 mm sterling silver sheet. Use a square file to make a crease in the middle. (See Diagram B on page 128.) File at least half the depth of the sheet. Bend to a 90° angle and use hard solder along the fold to reinforce the fragile bend.

3 Take another piece of the same material about 55 mm long for the curved edge of the inner frame. Form it into a smooth quarter circle around a bracelet mandrel, a large piece of pipe or a baseball bat. Trim, fit, and join the two pieces together, using silver hard solder. (See Diagram C on page 128.) Place the frame upside down on the back of the steel. With scribe, trace the interior of the frame onto the steel. Carefully saw out the shape, using a jeweler's saw. File edges and check the fit.

4 Take small sections of gold enamelists' foil and fold them into triple layers. Place and burnish each piece into the surface of the steel until the teeth bite into it. (See Diagram D on page 128.) Slowly heat from the back to get a deep black color on the steel. Let cool. For added color, place pieces of florist's foil on the surface, but do not fold, heat, or burnish, as it would remove the color. Secure the colored foil and seal the metal surface, by spraying 5–10 very light coats of matte varnish. Let dry between coats. Be certain to spray the sides and the back to prevent the steel from rusting.

5   Add a backing to portions of the inner frame to support the damascene piece. Cut slightly oversized sections of 0.5 mm sterling silver sheet; position and solder them to the frame with hard solder. Saw and file off the excess. (See Diagram E on page 128.)

6   Place the frame on a piece of 0.8 mm sterling silver sheet. Trace the outside of the inner "L" edge. Cut a piece of flat silver sheet to fit that angle. Set the dividers at 10 mm and scribe a flat "L" onto the sheet, 10 mm wide for the outer frame. Cut another piece of 1 mm x 6 mm sterling silver sheet about 150 mm long. Crease, fold, and solder this for the outer "L" edge. Place the three elements together upside down with the flat sheet supported halfway between what will be the front and back of the pin. Or press carefully and evenly into a charcoal block or block of plaster of paris. Solder from the back with medium solder. Be careful not to overheat or the previous hard solder joints may pull back. (See Diagram F on page 128.)

7   Secure the tubing in a large pin vise or tube vise. File the exposed end flat and then use a 3.5 mm setting bur to carve a seat into the end. When properly executed, the stone should fit snugly with about ¼ of the crown showing above the rim of the tubing. Remove the stone and cut off the tube/bezel at 5 mm (including the precut setting). Repeat for all four stones. (See Diagram G on page 129.)

Photo by Jerry Maddox

Bipartite Brooch #4

8   Use a saw or shear to cut out a group of little triangles and rectangles from the bimetal sheet. Flatten the pieces and file the edges. (See Diagram H on page 129.) Place the pieces on a soldering pad with the gold side downward. Flux and then put a few pieces of silver easy solder onto each and heat until it flows, covering the surface. If not already flat, file the bottoms of the tube settings and repeat the process of adding small chips of solder and then flowing it. Sand the bottoms of the shapes and tubes to level.

9   Place the elements on the outer frame and solder the tubes and flat shapes (gold side up) in place. Use a 1 mm bit to drill holes in the sheet, within the bases of the tube settings. (See Diagram I on page 129.)

10 Turn the piece over and affix the joint and catch in place with easy solder. (See Diagram J on page 129.) Clean and polish the silver mounting. Oxidize and repolish. Set the stones into the tube-bezels, using a burnisher, pusher, or punch. Add the nickel silver pin stem and hold it in place with a rivet, which is hammered to "upset" the ends. Put a few small dabs of silicone glue within the frame. Place the damascene plate in position and press down firmly.

PATRICK MURPHY

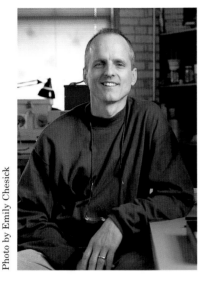

Photo by Emily Chesick

Photo by Ralph Gabriner

Blue & Green Pendant

Tadpoles, axolotls (immature salamanders, to the uninitiated), and red-eared sliders lured Patrick Murphy to the lakes and streams of southeastern Minnesota, where he grew up. College wasn't nearly as interesting as the outdoors, and Patrick dropped out during his second year. "I moved away from the city, as a part of the back-to-the-land migration of the early '70s, winding up in a tent on 120 acres of land in rural western Wisconsin. Then I realized that I needed a way to support myself in the place where I wanted to live."

As luck would have it, a friend showed Patrick a few silver rings he had made, which were set with lapis, carnelian, and agate. Patrick immediately recognized the same natural beauty he had found in reptiles and he was hooked. Intrigued enough to buy a few tools, Patrick tried making some jewelry on his own. In fact, Murphy Design's first studio was a tent.

As he learned more, he made and sold silver jewelry with tourmalines, opals, and other gems. His business evolved and Patrick began to take classes in art, design and gemology through the University of Minnesota, the Minneapolis College of Art and Design, the Gemological Institute of America, and the Revere Academy of Jewelry Arts.

Now a couple of decades later, Murphy Design is located in an historic building in downtown Minneapolis. Like all entrepreneurs, Patrick did most of the jobs himself before training others to help. Surrounded by a workshop full of tools and a small team of assistants, Patrick learned the ropes before handing the work off to someone else. But no matter how much he delegates, the studio is always a frenzy of activity centered around the artist. "At any one time I am designing a piece of jewelry while talking with a customer on the telephone, sorting through a parcel of stones, and answering questions from my workers," he confides. "I do not mind the excitement. I have a short attention span and I guess that is just the way that I work best."

Photo by Ralph Gabriner

Orange Druse Earrings

Photo by Ralph Gabriner

"I picked this piece of quartz for the symmetry and dendritic pattern of its inclusions," says Patrick.

DENDRITIC QUARTZ PENDANT

Materials		Measurements
14k	Yellow gold square wire	1.6 mm (14 gauge); 1.3 mm (16 gauge); 0.8 mm (gauge)
14k	Yellow gold sheet	0.6 mm (22 gauge); 0.5 (24 gauge); 0.3 mm (28 gauge) x 1 mm taller than stone
14k	Yellow gold tubing	Sized to match stones - 2 pieces
14k	White gold round wire	1.0 mm (18 gauge) round; 0.9 mm (19 gauge) round
	Dendritic quartz	
	Paraiba tourmaline	
	Diamond	

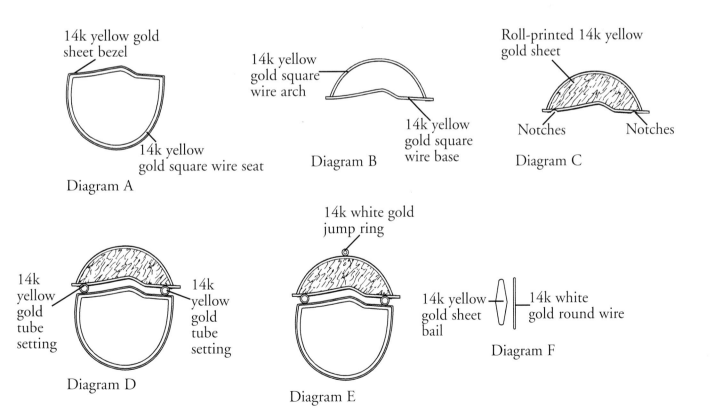

14k yellow gold sheet bezel

14k yellow gold square wire seat

Diagram A

14k yellow gold square wire arch

14k yellow gold square wire base

Diagram B

Roll-printed 14k yellow gold sheet

Notches   Notches

Diagram C

14k yellow gold tube setting

14k yellow gold tube setting

Diagram D

14k white gold jump ring

Diagram E

14k yellow gold sheet bail

14k white gold round wire

Diagram F

DENDRITIC QUARTZ PENDANT

Dendritic Druse Pendant

Photo by Ralph Gabriner

1 Form a strip of 0.3 mm gold sheet around the quartz. Cut the ends and join with yellow gold hard solder to make a bezel.

2 Cut a piece of 0.8 mm yellow gold square wire to fit inside the bezel as a seat for the stone. This leaves the setting with an open back so that light can pass through the translucent stone as well as conserve metal. Solder it in place with yellow gold hard solder. (See Diagram A on page 133.) File flat and finish the back of the bezel.

3 Form a piece of 1.6 mm gold square wire to match the contour of the top of the bezeled quartz. This forms the base of the top portion of the pendant. (See Diagram B on page 133.) Form an arch of 1.3 mm gold square wire to complement the shape of the bezeled quartz (i.e. to complete the oval shape). File the ends of the arch to fit the base, leaving about 2 mm on each end. Solder them with gold hard solder.

4 Roll-print a piece of 0.6 mm gold sheet for the inside of the top. Solder it to the back of the top assembly then file the edges flush. (See Diagram C on page 133.)

5 Select or make tubes for the two stones. Saw the tubing off 2 mm taller than the large bezel. Use a round needle file to make a half-round notch in the bottom piece to receive the tubes. (See Diagram C on page 133.) Solder tubes in notches flush with the back. Join the top section to the assembly. (See Diagram D on page 133.)

6 Use a 0.9 mm white gold round wire to form a jump ring. Use white gold medium solder to attach the jump ring to the top of the pendant. (See Diagram E on page 133.)

7 Cut the pattern for the bail from 0.5 mm gold sheet. Solder a piece of 0.8 mm yellow gold square wire down the middle of the bail. (See Diagram F on page 133.)

8 Solder the piece of 1.0 mm white gold round wire to the bail. Insert the other end of the wire through the jump ring at the top of the pendant. Bend the bail closed and solder.

9 Use setting burs to make seats for the small round stones, then use a pusher or punch to set them. Insert the quartz and push the bezel over.

10 Mask off all but the roll-printed recessed area with tape. Sandblast the exposed metal. Remove the tape. Polish and finish the pendant.

134

ROSS COPPELMAN

Photo by Adam Coppelman

"I never imagined that I would be making jewelry on Cape Cod for 27 years," says Ross Coppelman. Unlike many of his peers, Ross never felt a calling towards a career in the arts. "I wasn't mechanically inclined and artistic expression did not come naturally to me as a child." Ross had little idea at all what he would do with his life. "I was a spacey kid, adrift in a fog."

School was a difficult environment for what Ross calls his "disorganized ways," and despite coming from an academically oriented family, college was a challenge. After graduating from Harvard University, Ross needed something to do, and he had to find it quickly, otherwise graduate school was inevitable. Ross wanted a down-to-earth alternative to the competitive intellectual playing field where he had been all his life, both at home and at school. He imagined a career that he liked so much that going to work would be its own reward. By a stroke of good fortune, Ross fell into a job doing menial tasks for a production jeweler, knocking out silver rings for one dollar each. It wasn't much, but Ross liked the work. He took a deep breath and stepped back to examine the big picture. "Working as a jeweler gave me a great deal of satisfaction right from the start," he recalls. "I finally found something that I enjoyed doing, not just something that I had to do so that I could enjoy something else. Work and play became indistinguishable." That was back in the early 1970's and Ross has been playing ever since.

When he first struck out on his own, his jewelry was pretty simple, both in technique and in design. Ross's principle venue has been his own jewelry gallery on Cape Cod, which has continued to grow over the years.

Several years ago, Ross discovered the magic and allure of working in high-karat gold. Ross uses this metal and others to construct sculptural jewelry by fusing many pieces together. In this technique, the metal is placed in position and it is heated to a temperature below its flow point but above its melting point. There is an interval of heat in which it is possible to fuse (bond at the molecular level) the elements without solder. Although Ross plays down the artist's image, he uses his materials, precious metals, and gems, just as a painter would use the colors on his palette. Add a bit of gold here, a texture there, some diamonds and colored stones. Rearrange the gems, emphasize the negative space, and then evaluate the overall balance of the composition until everything finds its place. The only one who questions the artistry of his work is Ross himself. The rest of us, both wearers and viewers just stand back and appreciate the precious wearable art of Ross Coppelman.

Photo by Ralph Gabriner

Boulder Opal Pin II

BOULDER-OPAL PIN

Photo by Gene Baldi

This luxurious pin is typical of Ross' fused high-karat gold jewelry. It combines materials that emphasize dramatic color and textural differences. Since 22k gold is very soft, after the front is created it is mounted on a sturdier 18k yellow gold backing. In addition, because of its added strength, white gold is used for parts that take the most wear.

BOULDER-OPAL PIN

Materials		*Measurements*
22k	Yellow gold sheet	0.4 mm (26 gauge) x 3 mm wide
22k	Yellow gold round wire	1.3 mm (16 gauge)
18k	Yellow gold sheet	0.4 mm (26 gauge)
18k	White gold round wire	1 mm (18 gauge)
18k	White gold 4-prong settings	Sized to match diamonds - 4 pieces
	Boulder opal	
	Triangular diamond	1 piece
	Round diamonds	4 pieces
	Round cultured pearls	2 pieces
	Round button pearl	1 piece

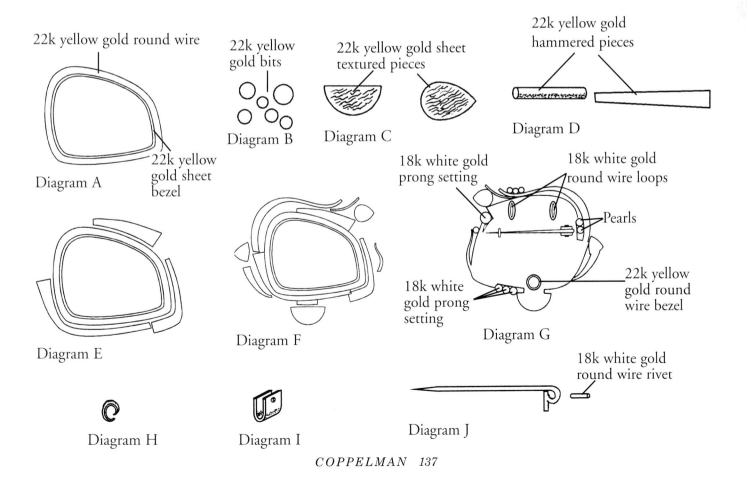

22k yellow gold round wire

22k yellow gold bits

22k yellow gold sheet textured pieces

22k yellow gold hammered pieces

22k yellow gold sheet bezel

Diagram A

Diagram B

Diagram C

Diagram D

18k white gold prong setting

18k white gold round wire loops

Pearls

18k white gold prong setting

22k yellow gold round wire bezel

Diagram E

Diagram F

Diagram G

18k white gold round wire rivet

Diagram H

Diagram I

Diagram J

BOULDER-OPAL PIN

1 Begin by wrapping a strip of 0.4 mm 22k gold sheet around the irregular boulder opal. Cut the material to fit, aligning the ends perfectly. Using very controlled heat, fuse the ends shut. (See Diagram A on page 137.) With a piece of 1.3 mm round wire, make a border for the bezel and fuse it shut. Double check the fit and fuse it to the base of the bezel.

2 Melt bits of 22k yellow gold of various sizes into an assortment of beads. Hammer some of these to flatten them into different shapes and sizes. Some are hammered with a knife-edge cross-peen hammer and some are reticulated (overheated to create irregular grainy surfaces). (See Diagram B on page 137.)

3 Make a half-round disk and pear-shaped piece, and texture with a metal stamp that has a zig-zag pattern. (See Diagram C on page 137.)

Photo by Ralph Gabriner

Lapis Lazuli Pin

4 Create other shapes by forging pieces of 22k gold round wire, stretching and forming them in random ways. Hammer some to create a dynamic tapered effect and then curve them to complement the shape of the opal. (See Diagram D on page 137.) Store extra forms for future jewelry. Strike the wires in selected spots with a knife-edged cross-peen hammer to create decorative lines in the gold.

5 Arrange the major elements around the center bezel. Use a large reducing flame to fuse the parts together at all contact points. (See Diagram E on page 137.)

6 Make a bezel for the triangular diamond from a 22k gold round wire. Experiment positioning the pearls and diamonds along with more of the hammered and fused 22k gold elements around the large opal to create an appealing design. Use a large reducing flame to fuse the parts together at the contact points. Add the rest of the 22k gold elements and fuse them in position. (See Diagram F on page 137.)

7 Place the 22k gold assembly onto an 18k gold sheet for backing. Join the two with 18k yellow gold hard solder. Reintroduce the negative spaces by drilling holes and sawing out the gold back plate. Trim the backing to conform with all the 22k gold details. File the edges smooth, sand and polish as necessary. Solder the 18k white gold prong settings and sections of 1 mm white gold wire to serve as pearl posts with hard solder. (See Diagram G on page 137.)

8 Use 1 mm white gold round wire to make two loops for the back, so that the piece can be

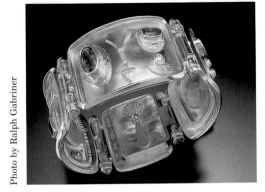

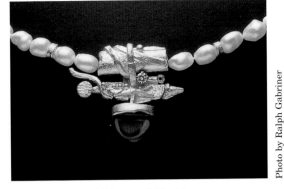

Tourmaline and Diamond Bracelet   *Tourmaline and Diamond Necklace*

Photo by Ralph Gabriner

Photo by Ralph Gabriner

worn on a chain. From the same wire, make a tight little "C" catch for the pin. (See Diagram H on page 137.) From the 18k gold sheet, cut out a rectangle, 4 mm wide and 12 mm long. Fold this over into a "U," leaving a 1 mm gap for the pin stem. Drill a 1 mm hole in both sides for a rivet. (See Diagram I on page 137.) Make a bezel for the 5 mm button pearl on the back from 22k yellow gold sheet. This supports the bottom of the pin so that the top cannot tip forward when worn. When arranging the pin mechanism, remember that looking at the back, the hinged joint goes on the right and the catch on the left. The loops, "C" catch, "U" joint, and bezel are all joined with medium solder, either all at once or individually.

9   Make a pin stem from 1 mm 18k white gold round wire. This should be hardened material, ideally from a piece of wire that has been drawn through many holes in a draw plate so that it is very springy. While it is still longer than necessary, bend one end into a tight loop, adding a tail that is perpendicular to the needle. Cut a piece of 1 mm 18k white gold round wire for the rivet. It should be about 1.5 mm longer than the outside width of the joint. (See Diagram J on page 137.)

10 Insert the pin stem into the joint. Push the rivet in place. Rotate the pin stem and cut it off so that it is 2 mm longer than the opening. As the pin is pushed down toward the catch, the tail stops the rotation around the rivet so that pressure must be exerted to force the pin stem down to the catch. Remove the rivet and pin stem. File the end to a taper and polish. Insert it for the final time. Insert the rivet. Place one end of the rivet on a steel anvil and use a cross-peen hammer or very small ball-peen hammer to upset the other end. Flip the pin around so that you can work alternately on both ends of the rivet until it is tight, but not so tight that the pin stem cannot rotate. Adjust the tail of the pin stem so that the tip rests about 3 mm away from the catch. Adjust the opening of the catch so that a very small amount of force is required to snap the pin in place.

11 Very lightly polish the entire piece. Set the diamonds with burs and a pusher. Because the bezels are made of 22k gold, it is very easy to move them over the stones. Use epoxy to glue the round pearls. Use a pusher to set the button pearl.

GLOSSARY

Bail — the loop or ring at the top of a pendant by which it hangs.

Ball peen — the spherical working end of a forming hammer.

Bead blasting — applying a fine surface texture by striking metal with small glass beads. The beads also harden and burnish the surface.

Bench jeweler — an artisan who works hands-on with tools to create or repair jewelry.

Bezel — a piece of metal wrapped around a stone and used to secure it in place.

Binding wire — traditionally made of soft blackened iron, this material is used to lash or otherwise hold pieces in place during soldering. Now, stainless steel binding wire is also available, with the advantage that it can be placed in the pickle without contamination.

Burnish — to hand or machine polish by rubbing a polished metal or stone tool against a metal surface.

Chamfer — to create a beveled or sloped corner. A beveled or sloped corner.

Chasing — to refine and apply fine detail to a surface with punches and a chasing hammer.

Chisel — a sharp steel tool used to cut softer metals, wood, bone, etc.

Counter enamel — applying enamel to the back of an object so that enamel on the front will not crack and break.

Crease — to bend along a scored line.

Die — a metal form into which sheet metal is pushed for forming. A blanking die made of steel is used to shear out a metal shape.

Escapement files — very small needle files.

Fibula — an ornamental and functional pin in which the mechanical elements are integral to the design.

Firescale — subsurface cupric oxide often appearing on sterling silver objects. It is the result of extended heating without protecting the surface with a substance like boric acid.

Flush cutters — a pair of cutting pliers or nippers which leaves a flat end.

Forging — hammering metal to change its cross section.

Forming — hammering metal to change its shape but not its cross section.

Goldsmith — traditionally, a person trained to work in gold. Contemporary meaning is any person skilled in making small objects, such as jewelry.

Grisaille — an enameling technique utilizing only black, white, and shades of grey.

Gum tragacanth — a natural gum used to hold powdered dry enamel in place.

Jeweler — an inclusive term describing a maker of jewelry, a maker of fine jewelry, or a merchant of jewelry.

Knife graver — a long narrow pointed graver used for fine work.

Lathe — a motor with a horizontal spindle or stock that holds material or tools when shaping metal.

Maker — one who loved to work with hands from an early age.

Makers' mark — the logo, trademark, or other identifying image which is generally applied to metal for identification.

Mandrel — a tapered shaft or rod around which metal is formed. Ring mandrels are used to measure, shape, and stretch rings.

Metalsmith — a collective term, meaning anybody who hammers or works metal, including goldsmiths, blacksmiths, silversmiths, etc.

Mild steel — a soft, low-carbon steel alloy.

Mushroom stake — a round ball-shaped stake used for creating large domed forms.

Niobium — one of three reactive metals that are colored by passing a current through them (anodic oxidation). The others are titanium and tantalum.

Onglette graver — a graver with a marquis cross section.

Paper die — a cut-out pattern in paper or thin board, which is roll-printed onto a metal surface.

Pickle — an acidic solution used to remove oxides and flux from metal. For jewelry, this often contains weak sulfuric acid.

Plastic abrasive pad — like a kitchen scouring pad, this useful item is excellent for brightening metal, applying a satin finish, cleaning metal surfaces, etc.

Platens — two flat plates that are forced closed in a press.

Ram — the piston-like part of a hydraulic press that moves up and down, closing the platens.

Reciprocating hammer hand piece — an attachment for the flexible-shaft machine with a motor-driven impacting tip. It is used for stone setting, engraving, and riveting.

Ring blank — a strip of metal used to form a ring.

Rivets — pins used to mechanically join components without heat or solder.

Sandblasting — applying a very fine texture, when sand is forced through a blasting nozzle.

Score — to scribe a deep line into sheet or wire.

Silhouette die — a die consisting of the outline or silhouette of a desired object. Metal can be sheared to the same outline as the die.

Silicon carbide — an abrasive grit that is embedded into paper or cloth.

Silversmith — traditionally, a person trained to work in silver, creating larger vessels with hammers. Contemporary meaning is any person making jewelry out of silver.

Spindle — a threaded, tapered shaft upon which a rotating wheel is mounted.

Split-lap machine — a sophisticated horizontal polishing lathe for finishing metal. A hard felt wheel with slits is mounted on a tapered spindle to permit viewing the surface being polished.

Spring gauge — a spring-action caliper that measures thickness of wire or sheet.

Sweat soldering — joining components by first flowing solder on one part and then assembling it with the other, followed by heating so that the solder joins to the second part.

Upset — to flare the end of a rivet by hammering.

Urethane — a synthetic rubber-like material, which is available in a range of hardness and dimension.

Photo by Ralph Gabriner

DEAN

METRIC CONVERSION CHART

Inch	Millimetre	B&S gauge	Drill number	Inch	Millimetre	B&S gauge	Drill number	Inch	Millimetre	B&S gauge	Drill number
0.001	0.025			0.040	1.016	18	60	0.079	2.007		47
0.002	0.051			0.041	1.041		59	0.080	2.032		
0.003	0.076	40		0.042	1.067		58	0.081	2.057	12	46
0.004	0.102	38		0.043	1.092		57	0.082	2.083		45
0.005	0.127	36		0.044	1.118			0.083	2.108		
0.006	0.152	34	97	0.045	1.143	17		0.084	2.134		
0.007	0.178	33	94	0.046	1.168			0.085	2.159		
0.008	0.203	32	92	0.047	1.194		56	0.086	2.184		44
0.009	0.229	31	89	0.048	1.219			0.087	2.210		
0.010	0.254	30	87	0.049	1.245			0.088	2.235		
0.011	0.279	29	85	0.050	1.270			0.089	2.261		43
0.012	0.305	28	83	0.051	1.295	16		0.090	2.286		
0.013	0.330		81	0.052	1.321		55	0.091	2.311	11	
0.014	0.356	27	80	0.053	1.346			0.092	2.337		
0.015	0.381		79	0.054	1.372			0.093	2.362		
0.016	0.406	26	78	0.055	1.397		54	0.094	2.388		42
0.017	0.432			0.056	1.422			0.095	2.413		
0.018	0.457	25	77	0.057	1.448	15		0.096	2.438		41
0.019	0.483			0.058	1.473			0.097	2.464		
0.020	0.508	24	76	0.059	1.499			0.098	2.489		40
0.021	0.533		75	0.060	1.524		53	0.099	2.515		
0.022	0.559	23	74	0.061	1.549			0.100	2.540		39
0.023	0.584			0.062	1.575			0.102	2.591		10
0.024	0.610		73	0.063	1.600			0.114	2.896		9
0.025	0.635	22	72	0.064	1.626	14	52	0.128	3.251		8
0.026	0.660		71	0.065	1.651			0.144	3.658		7
0.027	0.686			0.066	1.676			0.162	4.115	6	
0.028	0.711	21	70	0.067	1.702		51	0.182	4.623	5	
0.029	0.737		69	0.068	1.727			0.204	5.182	4	
0.030	0.762			0.069	1.753			0.229	5.817	3	
0.031	0.787		68	0.070	1.778		50	0.258	6.553	2	
0.032	0.813	20	67	0.071	1.803			0.289	7.341	1	
0.033	0.838		66	0.072	1.829	13					
0.034	0.864		65	0.073	1.854		49				
0.035	0.889			0.074	1.880						
0.036	0.914	19	64	0.075	1.905						
0.037	0.940		63	0.076	1.930		48				
0.038	0.965		62	0.077	1.956						
0.039	0.991		61	0.078	1.981						

INDEX